METAMERICANA

METAMERICANA

SETH ABRAMSON

BLAZEVOX[BOOKS]

Buffalo, New York

Metamericana
by Seth Abramson
Copyright © 2015

Published by BlazeVOX [books]

Printed in the United States of America

Interior design and typesetting by Geoffrey Gatza
Cover Art by Sheila Wallis ("Head of a Boxer")

First Edition
ISBN: 978-1-60964-194-8
Library of Congress Control Number: 2014954647

BlazeVOX [books]
131 Euclid Ave
Kenmore, NY 14217

Editor@blazevox.org

publisher of weird little books

BlazeVOX [books]

blazevox.org

21 20 19 18 17 16 15 14 13 12 01 02 03 04 05 06 07 08 09 10

BlazeVOX

TABLE OF CONTENTS

A Note on the Text

Metamericana comprises original, appropriated, and remixed material. Each work is the result of a conceptual constraint; brief descriptions of some of these constraints can be found at the back of the collection.

METAMERICANA

AUTOBIOGRAPHICAL NOTE

Trigger warning for 9/11. Trigger warning for ableism. Trigger warning for abusive relationship. Trigger warning for ageism. Trigger warning for alcoholism. Trigger warning for amputation. Trigger warning for animal abuse. Trigger warning for animal death. Trigger warning for animal violence. Trigger warning for blood (gore). Trigger warning for blood (minor). Trigger warning for bodies/corpses. Trigger warning for bones (animal). Trigger warning for bullying. Trigger warning for car accident. Trigger warning for child abuse. Trigger warning for childbirth. Trigger warning for classism. Trigger warning for cyberbullying. Trigger warning for death/dying. Trigger warning for death penalty. Trigger warning for dental trauma. Trigger warning for domestic abuse (emotional). Trigger warning for domestic abuse (physical). Trigger warning for domestic abuse (sexual). Trigger warning for domestic abuse (verbal). Trigger warning for drinking (recreational). Trigger warning for drug use (intravenous). Trigger warning for drug use (prescription). Trigger warning for ED (anorexia). Trigger warning for ED (binge eating). Trigger warning for ED (bulimia). Trigger warning for fatphobia. Trigger warning for forced captivity. Trigger warning for graphic sex. Trigger warning for guns. Trigger warning for Holocaust (discussion). Trigger warning for Holocaust (images). Trigger warning for homophobia. Trigger warning for hospitalization. Trigger warning for hostages. Trigger warning for hunting. Trigger warning for incest. Trigger warning for insects. Trigger warning for kidnapping. Trigger warning for medical procedures. Trigger warning for misgendering. Trigger warning for murder. Trigger warning for murder (attempted). Trigger warning for Nazism. Trigger warning for needles. Trigger warning for overdose (accidental). Trigger warning for overdose (fatal). Trigger warning for overdose (intentional). Trigger warning for pedophilia. Trigger warning for poisoning. Trigger warning for pregnancy. Trigger warning for prostitution. Trigger warning for PTSD. Trigger warning for racism. Trigger warning for rape. Trigger warning for rape (attempted). Trigger warning for scarification. Trigger warning for self-harm (cutting). Trigger warning for serious injury. Trigger warning for sexism. Trigger warning for sexual abuse. Trigger warning for skeletons. Trigger warning for skulls. Trigger warning for slurs. Trigger warning for smoking. Trigger warning for snakes. Trigger warning for spiders. Trigger warning for suicidal thoughts. Trigger warning for suicide. Trigger warning for suicide (attempted). Trigger warning for swearing. Trigger warning for terminal illness. Trigger warning for terrorism. Trigger warning for transphobia. Trigger warning for trigger warnings. Trigger warning for violence. Trigger warning for vomit. Trigger warning for warfare.

I

GENESIS

Much made of little. Little made of knowledge. Knowledge made of scholarship. Scholarship made of textbooks. Textbooks made of terms. Terms made of semesters. Semesters made of weeks. Weeks made of days. Days made of decisions. Decisions made of mistakes. Mistakes made of love. Love made of mistakes. Mistakes made of blindness. Blindness made of darkness. Darkness made of curtains. Curtains made of dresses. Dresses made of flags. Flags made of nations. Nations made of wars. Wars made of beliefs. Beliefs made of Bibles. Bibles made of envelopes. Envelopes made of dust jackets. Dust jackets made of manuscripts. Manuscripts made of skin. Skin made of genetics. Genetics made of chromosomes. Chromosomes made of DNA. DNA made of nucleotides. Nucleotides made of adenine. Adenine made of $C_5H_5N_5$. $C_5H_5N_5$ made of molecules. Molecules made of atoms. Atoms made of protons, neutrons, and electrons. Protons and neutrons made of quarks and gluons. Quarks and gluons made of guesses. Guesses made of uncertainty. Uncertainty made of humanity. Humanity made of God. God made of Bibles. Bibles made of paper. Paper made of trees. Trees made of wood. Wood made of rings. Rings made of silver. Silver made of moonlight. Moonlight made of fantasy. Fantasy made of cleverness. Cleverness made of ridicule. Ridicule made of Hondas. Hondas made of steel. Steel made of Superman. Superman made of Marvel. Marvel made of DC. DC made of politicians. Politicians made of turkey. Turkey made of banks. Banks made of efficacy. Efficacy made of ink. Ink made of blood. Blood made of chocolate. Chocolate made of God. God made of Bibles. Bibles made of laws. Laws made of men. Men made of women. Women made of women. Women made of women. Women made of women. Women made of women. Women made of women. Women made of women. Women made of women.

We're like Anthony and Cleopatra. We're like Lewis and Clark. We're like Leopold and Loeb. We're like Abbott and Costello. We're like Gilbert and Sullivan. We're like John and Paul. We're like John and Yoko. We're like Sonny and Cher. We're like Ike and Tina. We're like Diana and Dodi. We're like Thelma and Louise. We're like Jay and Silent Bob. We're like Batman and Robin. We're like Holmes and Watson. We're like Bert and Ernie. We're like Ken and Barbie. We're like Bugs and Daffy. We're like Beavis and Butthead. We're like Tweedle Dee and Tweedle Dum. We're like Hansel and Gretel. We're like Dick and Jane.

We're like Jack and Jill. We're like Jan & Dean. We're like Simon & Garfunkel. We're like Captain & Tennille. We're like Cheech & Chong. We're like Donny & Marie. We're like Hall & Oates. We're like Starsky & Hutch. We're like Mork & Mindy. We're like Laverne & Shirley. We're like Penn & Teller. We're like Bill & Ted. We're like Ben & Jerry. We're like Tom & Jerry. We're like Chip & Dale. We're like Ren & Stimpy. We're like Pinky & the Brain. We're like Itchy & Scratchy. We're like Terrance & Phillip.

We're like Rocky & Bullwinkle. Like Bonnie and Clyde. Like Harold and Maude. Like Regis and Kathie Lee. Like Arnold and Willis. Like Zach and Screech. Like Urkel and Laura. Like Will and Carlton. Like Dorian and Turk. Like Jim and Dwight. Like Karen and Jack. Like Sam and Neal. Like George and Barbara. Like Robert and Claudia. Like all my exes and me.

Like AT&T. S&M. T&A. M&M. A&E. B&N. S&P. A&M. D&D. A&P. B&B. P&G. P&J. R&R. D&G. H&M. M&A. A&F. P&W. B&E. A&S. W&M. J&J. B&O.

OMG. CEO. IBM. FYI. TMI. FAQ. KKK. MLB. GMC. TNT. TSA. DOA. MMA. DWI. EMT. FCC. LLC. AIG. XXX. PVC. PNC. ENT. NIH. TWA. RPI. TDK. AGI. OMB. US.

ID. AC. TD. IQ. HD. GE. FX. GQ. DQ. AA. NA. BJ. BM. MD. KO. ET. OD. AI. LP. RN. IP. VD. YA. AV. EZ. XX. NH. MS. JP. LB. SB. PA. WC. MJ. AD.

CC. Id. Pi. Bi. Ed. Op. Lo. Da. Ba. Ay. Oy. Um. Uh. Ah. Hm. Mm. Er. Eh. Aw. Om. Sh.

THE HISTORY OF DAIRY QUEEN

- 1939: Hitler invades Poland.
- 1940: First Dairy Queen® store opens in Joliet, Illinois.
- 1949: DQ® introduces malts and shakes.
- 1951: Banana splits appear on the DQ® menu.
- 1953: First DQ® store opens in Canada.
- 1955: The Dilly® Bar debuts.
- 1957: The Dairy Queen®/Brazier® concept is introduced.
- 1958: Dairy Queen®/Brazier® food products are introduced.
- 1961: The Mr. Misty® slush treat cools throats in the warm South.
- 1962: International Dairy Queen, Inc. (IDQ) is formed.
- 1965: First radio advertising sends out DQ® message 169 million times weekly.
- 1966: First national TV commercial, "Live a Little," is aired.
- 1968: The Buster Bar® Treat bursts forth.
- 1972: First DQ® store opens in Japan.
- 1973: Say "Scrumpdillyishus®!" and get a Peanut Buster® Parfait for 49¢.
- 1979: The DQ® system debuts in the Middle East.
- 1980: "We Treat You Right®" tagline debuts.
- 1985: More than 175 million Blizzard® Treats sold in its first year.
- 1989: Dairy Queen® ranked America's number one treat chain.
- 1991: First DQ® store opens in Mexico.
- 1995: DQ® Treatzza Pizza® and Chicken Strip Basket make their debuts.
- 1999: Pecan Mudslide® Treat is introduced.
- 1999: A DQ® operator builds the world's largest blended treat (5,316.6 pounds).
- 2001: Crispy Chicken Salad is introduced.
- 2001: The first DQ Grill & Chill® restaurant opens in Chattanooga, Tennessee.
- 2002: Dallas Mavericks owner Mark Cuban manages a Texas DQ® for the day.
- 2003: The Blizzard® of the Month program kicks off.
- 2004: The MooLatte® Frozen Coffee Flavored Beverage line debuts.
- 2004: Award-winning DQ® commercials can be seen throughout the country.
- 2005: GrillBurgers™ are introduced to consumers on national TV.
- 2005: On June 21, a new World's Largest Blizzard® Treat is built in Springfield, Massachusetts. It weighs 8,224.85 pounds and is 22 feet tall.

#SADTOYS

Careless Bears. Not Wheels. Gobots. Optimus Meh. Tickle-Me Eeyore. Speak and Autocorrect. Mr. Pothead. Arby's Dream House. Taser Tag. Managed Care Bears. Upper G.I. Joe. Where Did He Touch You Elmo. Tickle Me Emo. Risk-Averse. Solitaire Confinement. Serf Village. Microscopic Machines. Speak and Dwell.

Simon Begs. Garfunkel Says. Raggedy Andy Dick. Sobby Horse. Barbie Dream Doublewide. Her Little Pony. Average Average Princess. Etsy Sketch. Baby's First Dali. Easy Bake Dutch Oven. Goodbye Kitty. Chatty Catheter. The #Sadtoys game is very revealing of your age, FYI. Sullen Putty. Mr. Potato. Rainbow Spite. FIFA 1939. Teenage Mutant Ninjas. Sitar Hero. Lego Pompeii. Lego Alderaan. Mii. Ping. Yo. Mousse Trap. Sad toys are dirty ones; remember that, ladies. Gobots. (Amirite?)

Nixon Logs. Pogs. Ex-box. XBox 180. Sega Saturn. Sega Leviticus. Sega Dreamcast. Settlers for Catan. Oregon Trail. (Seriously, go back and play it—everyone dies of terrible shit.) Hungry Hungry Humans. France France Revolution. Matchbox Le Cars. Civil War Operation. Operation: Iraqi Freedom. Army Men on Leave. Junior Shake Weight. Tragic Eightball. Class-Action Figures. iTouchy. Sim Detroit. Top10 #Trending Topics: 1: #SadToys 2: #CraigforCongress 3: #ThisCouldBeUsButImFat #RedNation #wcw #MattsVideoOftheWeek Sorry, This Doesn't Usually Happen.

Really Sorry! Unsuccessful Operation. Inoperable. Life With An Incurable Disease. Autopsy. A Ouija board to bring dad back. The good die young, and the ungrateful have everything. Cribbage. Pick-up Stick. Kick the Crayon. Don't Wake Stepdaddy.

Jumped rope. Toystore-bought musical instruments. A recorder. My First Crucifix. Dreidels. Yellow snow. A dead bird you found down by the creek. Toy boats that can't float. An empty refrigerator. Books. Money. A stick. My dick. Sidewalk chalk outlines. A bag of broken glass. My stepmother's lighter. Mouse crap. Cigarettes. A bowl of condoms. A dirty extension cord. Some bullshit, handcrafted wooden toy (when my friends all got Nintendos). Colorful household cleaners. Dolls made of Kleenex. A phone cord tied to a hairbrush. A pill bottle. Rocks. Broken glass. Jump rope and a stool. Plastic bags. A knife. Shopping for a car in Wichita? 2013 Suzuki SX4 Sportback Base Hatchback. Please Read and Share: "Such a Waste: Don't Let Fame Take You By Surprise, Prepare for It!" My heart. Your imagination.

HOW LONG IT TAKES

Your Yahoo! group receives your message. A cash deposit at an ATM clears. A laser treatment for cellulite achieves results. A DS1 communication is detected by planetary receivers. Moonlight reaches Earth. Your MCAT scores are sent through THx to a institutional recipient. A bounced email appears in your in-box.

Changes to your CloudFlare zone push out. Your nail polish dries. Participants in a SurveyMonkey survey receive their invitation. A spider finishes spinning its web. Your Viagra kicks in. Your Cialis kicks in.

Your SSL installation concludes. Hormone uptake from your removed Nuva Ring ceases. Your LinkedIn ad is approved. The chao in your *Sonic Adventure 2* game evolves. Your dog's Frontline application begins killing fleas. Consumed food is incorporated into your breast milk.

Your ejaculated sperm fertilizes a female egg. An online bill payment reaches your biller. Your webpage is listed as "protected" under the Protected Pages list in the DMCA Protection Portal. Your receive a badge for being especially helpful to users of the Meta Stack Exchange.

DNS propagation completes. Nicotine leaves your bloodstream after the cessation of your smoking habit. Your diflucan kicks in. Your muscles begin recovery after a prolonged and strenuous workout. A check deposit at an ATM clears. Google Places updates newly verified listings, business names, addresses, phone numbers, website URLs, descriptions, pin marker moves, and categories. Corrections to your FAFSA are processed. A turkey thaws. A small canyon is formed. Stripe payments are transferred to your bank account. The quick of your dog's nail recedes after a trimming of the tip. A Hepatitis B virus, lacking a human host, becomes inert. Google Places updates your photos and videos.

Your breast milk dries up after the cessation of breast-feeding. A database of cell phone towers is updated. Your Fiverr payment clears. A bird egg hatches. Google Places updates your duplicate and merged listings. Soft tissue heals after a tooth extraction. Your approved student loan is disbursed. Marijuana leaves your bloodstream. Your Amazon Visa rewards card points get credited. A credit transaction is reported to a credit reporting agency. A credit card payment is reported to a credit reporting agency. You begin to ovulate after removing your Nuva Ring.

The tomatoes you planted are ready to be harvested. A corporate merger goes through. A black hole consumes an object that originated at a point in space a hundred million miles distant. Your cat gives birth to a new litter. Your Hepatitis B completes its incubation period. An African child whose education and nourishment you sponsor receives your letter. Your divorce becomes final. Retinoids begin beneficially affecting the quality of your skin. You finish healing from your dental implant procedure. A hen begins laying eggs. A medical debt is sent to collection.

The IRS approves an organization's 501(c)(3) status. Plastic photodegrades. The period for cashing in EE savings bonds begins. Your damaged credit progresses to "fair," and you receive an unsecured credit card in the mail.

Epilepsy becomes intractable. HIV develops into AIDS. A genetically modified food product passes governmental safety tests and appears in stores nationwide.

Secondary-progressive Multiple Sclerosis develops.

An animal fossilizes.

Plastic biodegrades.

THINGS IN LOS ANGELES TONIGHT

Source: Merriam-Webster Dictionary

Kings, queens, princesses, swords, bows, arrows, staves, horses, doublets, tridents, daggers, stilettos, axes, clubs, Mace, Lances, partisans, ships, pike, slings, spears, assassins, magicians, thieves, rogues, clerics, soldiers, knights, bishops, pawns, crowns, flags, banners, trolls, ogres, fools, dwarves, bards, brownies, harps, lutes, gowns, wizards, fairies, deer, legends, hunters, rangers, wolves, poisons, pixies, muses, Sprites, elves, hags, witches, imps, wanderers, nomads, devils, farriers, fletchers, cobblers, jesters, spirits, haunts, inns, barkeeps, sailors, mutton, vampires, harpies, hounds, satyrs, sphinxes, sirens, gargoyles, incubuses, serpents, chimeras, golems, ghouls, skeletons, tombs, Cyclops, heroes, villains, Drakes, gorgons, nymphs, virgins, ballads, dungeons, whips, gremlins, angels, myths, behemoths, monsters, Griffins, man-eaters, hellhounds, outlaws, Raiders, mummies, doppelgangers, zombies, travelers, *Poltergeist*, *Leprechaun*, fantasies, aliens, lasers, cowboys, Indians, robots, explorers, spacecraft, gamma rays, chivalry, ghoulishness, gigantism, caves, mincemeat, *Joust*, Fireballs, acrobats, portals, maps, adventurers, role-playing, characters, modules, manuals, dice. A knife in the back and a death by fire.

TWENTY UNRELATED BUT TRUE STATEMENTS
ABOUT WEST LONDON IN 1999

— This place is too crowded.

— It feels like a perfect night to dress up like hipsters.

— It seems like one of those nights we should ditch the whole scene.

— It feels like one of those nights we won't be sleeping.

— We'll end up dreaming instead of sleeping.

— It feels like a perfect night for breakfast at midnight.

— There are too many cool kids here.

— Everything will be all right if we just keep dancing.

— It feels like a perfect night to fall in love with strangers.

— We're happy, free, confused, and lonely at the same time.

— Everything will be all right if you keep me next to you.

— I don't know about you, but I'm feeling twenty-two.

— You look like bad news.

— Tonight's the night we forget about deadlines.

— Tonight's the night we forget about heartbreaks.

— It's miserable and magical.

— It feels like a perfect night to make fun of our exes.

— ...

— ...

— You don't know about me, but I bet you want to.

— I've got to have you.

— It's time.

THE TOP 50 MOMENTS OF THE 2014 WINTER OLYMPICS

(written in real time between February 7th and February 23rd, 2014)

This one.

This one.

This one.

This one.

This one.

This one.

This one.

This one.

This one.

This one.

This one.

This one.

This one.

This one.

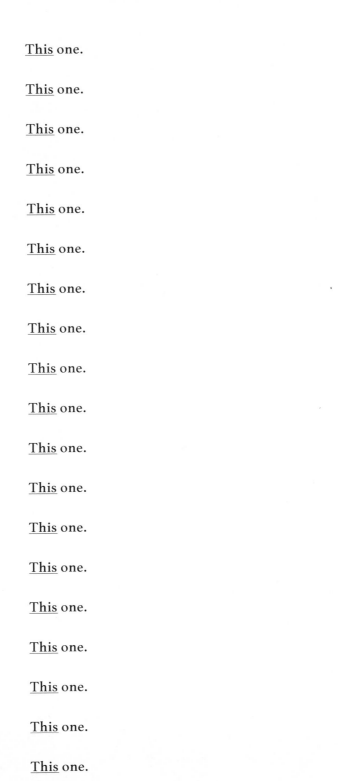

This one.

This one.

This one.

This one.

This one.

This one.

This one.

This one.

This one.

This one.

This one.

This one.

This one.

This one.

This one.

This one.

This one.

This one.

<u>This</u> one.

<u>This</u> one.

<u>This</u> one.

<u>This</u> one.

<u>This</u> one.

<u>This</u> one.

<u>This</u> one.

<u>This</u> one.

<u>This</u> one.

<u>This</u> one.

<u>This</u> one.

<u>This</u> one.

<u>This</u> one.

<u>This</u> one.

<u>This</u> one.

And this one.

ZERO KOOL

The recovery of the world economy may very well depend on science finding a way to harness the power of the Cuil (/'ku:l/KOOL).

Cuil theory is cutting edge.

Advances in the field of Cuil theory are occurring at an unheard-of pace.

Cuil theory lampoons the search engine capabilities of the Cuil search engine, while providing a functional and intellectually stimulating framework for considering the interrelationship of tangents.

Example: You ask me for a hamburger.

-1 Cuil: Postmodernism.

0 Cuil: You ask me for a hamburger. I hand you the epitome of a hamburger, down to the most minute detail. Note that humans inhabiting a 0 Cuil state experience the Cuil Paradox, in which the ratio of asked-for and received hamburger is so close to 1:1 that reality is no longer plausible.

1 Cuil: You ask me for a hamburger. I give you a raccoon.

2 Cuils: You ask me for a hamburger, but I don't exist. Where once I stood sits a picture of a hamburger.

3 Cuils: You awake as a hamburger. The world is in sepia.

4 Cuils: Why are we speaking German? A mime whimpers as he cradles a young cow. Your grandfather stares at you. The cow falls apart into patties. You look down to see me sitting on the ground. I have pickles for eyes. I sing a song that gives birth to the universe.

5 Cuils: You ask for a hamburger. I give you a hamburger. You raise it to your lips and take a bite. Your eye twitches involuntarily. Across the street a father of three falls down the stairs. You swallow and look down at the hamburger in your hands. I give you a hamburger. You swallow and look down at the hamburger in your hands. You cannot swallow. There are children at the top of the stairs. A pickle shifts uneasily under the bun. I give you a hamburger. You look at my face, and I begin to plead with you. The children are crying now. You raise the hamburger to your lips. Tears stream down your face as you take a bite. I give you a hamburger. You are on your knees. You plead with me to go across the street. I hear only children's laughter. I give you a hamburger. You are screaming as you fall down the stairs. I am your child. You cannot see anything. You take a bite of the hamburger. The concrete rushes up to meet you. You awake with a start in your own bed. Your eye twitches involuntarily. I give you a hamburger. I make no sound when you kill me. I give you a hamburger.

6 Cuils: You ask me for a hamburger. My response is cut short as all electrons are removed from my body. Across a variety of hidden dimensions, you are dismayed. John Lennon hands me an apple, but it slips through my fingers. I am reborn as an ocelot. You disapprove. A crack echoes through the universe in defiance of physics. Cosmological background noise shifts from randomness to a perfect A-flat. Children everywhere stop what they are doing and hum along. Birds fall from the sky as the sun engulfs the earth. You hesitate, then allow yourself to become the locus of all knowledge. Entropy crumbles as you peruse the hard data of the universe. A small library in Phoenix ceases to exist. You stumble under the weight of all extant masses. Your mouth opens up to cry out, then collapses around your body. You depart a particular spatial plane. You exist only in the fourth dimension. The fountainhead of all knowledge rolls along the ground and collides with a small dog. My head tastes sideways as space-time is reestablished. You blink back into the corporeal world disoriented. I hand you a hamburger as my body collapses under the strain of its reconstitution. The universe reasserts itself. A particular small dog is fed steak for the rest of its natural life. You die in a freak accident. Your spirit inhabits the returns desk of the Phoenix Public Library. You disapprove. Your disapproval sends ripples through the dimensional void between Life and Death. A small child begins to cry as he walks toward the stairway where his father stands.

7 Cuils: I give you a hamburger. The universe is engulfed within itself. A bus advertising hot dogs drives by a Papillon. It disapproves. An unknown force reverses Earth's gravity. You ask for a hamburger. I reply by handing you a mildly convulsing potato. You disapprove. Your disapproval enacts a cosmic shift in the void between Life and Birth. You ask for a hamburger. A particular small dog feasts on hamburger patties for the remainder of its unnaturally long lifespan. Your constant disapproval sends silence through everything. A contrived beast becomes omnipotent. You ask for a hamburger. I give you a hamburger. Your body is a shivering blob of nothingness that slowly divides into three parts. The Papillon barks. The universe realigns itself. You, the Papillon, and the hamburger disapprove. This condemnation stops the realignment. Hades freezes. A pig is launched by a specific hamburger into the unoccupied existence between space and time. You ask for a hamburger. I disapprove and condemn you to an eternity in a certain void where a certain pig and its specific hamburger are now located. You are locked away and are fed hamburgers for the rest of your natural life. A pickle refuses to break down during the process of digestion. You die in a freak accident. A certain pickle lives the rest of its natural life in a comatose state. Your spirit disapproves. Down the street a child cries as a hamburger gets stuck in her esophagus. You ask again for a hamburger. I refuse to hand you one. I remind you that this is the New World Order. Only Papillons exist now. You demand legal representation. Your name is added to a list of sins. Blasphemy. You ask for a hamburger. Realignment begins. You beg for a hamburger. A certain Papillon's name is written on an obelisk in Egypt. Mumble. Peasants worship the obelisk. Your corpse dances. Hamburgers are banned worldwide. The sun implodes. The planets never existed. Mercury. Venus. Earth. Mars. Jupiter. Saturn. Uranus. Neptune. Pluto is the only mass remaining. You are on vacation there. Your hunger for a hamburger reestablishes space-time. Earth is reborn under your rule. Hamburgers are your army.

You wake up.

Clowns. Clowns everywhere.

II

POEM

"So, in a nation in which face-to-face interaction in general and public oration specifically is becoming less and less common, and in which the opportunity to speak to a group of people about art is even less common than that, I'm going to perform for you now some joyless, self-aggrandizing, derivative ephemera? Instead of telling you that (a) poets are the very worst readers and synthesizers of poetry, as they feel the most entitled to its history but are by far the least avid or tutored consumers of that history; (b) American poetry in particular is suffused with a terminal smugness born of the cultural oblivion to which it has willfully, self-righteously, even orgasmically confined itself; (c) avant-garde poetry in America has, in plain view and for forty years now, been the stillborn bastard of careerist scholars in the American academy, its ambitions so lifeless that even those who crow about it on social media and at listless circle-jerk quasi-scholarly conferences can't be bothered to even *pretend* to harbor any plausible enthusiasm for it, it's [sic] readers, or its ostensible ideological underpinnings, other than to hope upon hope that some turgid nugget of Continental theory or warmed-over Cagean experiment they orate at a Bed-Stuy cookout next month will somehow score them half a page in the third edition of the *Norton Anthology of Postmodern American Poetry*; (d) worst of all are the many purveyors of so-called "experimental writing," who obscure their provincial and retrograde formal biases with a skin-deep commitment to risk that somehow never arouses a modicum of emotional consternation or the slightest suspicion of real courage from any reader anywhere; and finally (e) all of the above is performed with such noxious, nauseating faux sincerity and/or fey irony that it's become impossible to believe that any poet still uses daily and with such simpering good cheer the very social media platforms that are so evidently killing their spirit, their ambition, and their clarity of vision regarding the only abidingly important task art has allotted them: fucking with not just literary but cultural conventions.

Fine.

Fine.

Here's a poem."

METAPOETICA

Dear Poetry Ma Poem to be read silently. Poem to be muttered. Poem to cut. Poem to be read by two people simultaneously. Poem to be read by a twelve year-old black girl in Jackson, Mississippi. Poem to be read only once. Poem to be read while "Sister Christian" plays. Poem to be played on a water park loudspeaker. Poem not to be read. Poem to be mailed to an address in Georgia. Poem to be read at half speed. Poem to be memorized and recited to a mirror. Poem to burn after reading. Poem to gain entry to Marquee *I hope you will con* on 10th Avenue. Poem to fall from love to. Poem to stain with coffee and tea. Poem to sustain interest in a subway wall. Poem to be read after yoga. Poem to prop your table. Poem to pay your bill. Poem to be read by my mother if I die first. Poem to staple to a hand. Poem to save a life. Poem to hamper. *from my fourth man* Poem to cue your memory of a clearing in a garden. Poem to sit you down. Poem to snarl. Poem to tear at the corners of. Poem to snivel. Poem to resurrect a conversation *been working in a new paradigm* in a fogged-up Honda behind your house. Poem to throw in water. Poem to be read by a priest to a parishioner, and a parishioner to a child, and a child to an imaginary friend, and that friend to no one. Poem to hold in a hospital bed. Poem to be read after dark. Poem to be read with breakfast. Poem to be texted. Poem to be reviewed for tenure. *I realize. But I believe that* Poem in the hopper. Poem to disappear after seven seconds. Poem to be read by friends and followers and subscribers only. Poem to be left at the door of a stranger. Poem to get her back. Poem to keep in the back of your wallet. Poem to be left on the printer at work. Poem to quit to. Poem to be misread. Poem to be remixed.

Poem to apologize. Poem to be kept at the bank. Poem to be inherited. Poem to be published by *The New York Times* as a Letter to the Editor. Poem to risk execution for *and metamodernism may be*. Poem that might have been. Poem to stuff in a bottle at sea. Poem to stuff in a bottle and light and throw. Poem to land with a reader fifty years on. Poem to be fished from the trash. Poem to be close-read. Poem stolen. Poem. Poem to be workshopped. Poem to shred. Poem. Poem to be read by a Nazi sympathizer *Thank you for your time* in Argentina. Poem published and retracted. Poem. Poem to be read by my father when I disappoint him. Poem. Poem to eulogize. Poem as Joaquin Phoenix. Poem as Pol Pot. Poem on the fifty-third page of the first draft of your screenplay, adapted from page 209 of your novel. Poem. Poem. Poem to be translated into Urdu. Poem. Poem to be read by a news anchor. Poem. Poem disavowed. Poem. Poem to ward off disaster at sea. Poem. Poem. Poem to celebrate a holiday you don't celebrate. Poem. Poem. Poem. Poem to gift. Poem. Poem to steal. Poem. Poem to leave on a pillow. Poem to sleep on. Poem. Poem to be dreamt. Poem. Poem to poet. Poem. Poem to posterity. Poem. Poem. Poem forgotten. Poem. Poem. Poem. Poem. Poem. Poem to be sung. Poem. Poem. Poem to be shouted. Poem. Poem. Poem. Poem. Poem. Poem to march to, *Seth Abramson*.

WHO IS SETH ABRAMSON?

I.

In March of 1776, wee robots appeared in Concord, Massachusetts.
Composed entirely of tools, they searched suburban American farms
for mass murderer Lance Cole. On March 12th, he was found riding
in the woods. His last words: "Shun biography! Learn _is_! Learn _of_!"

Northerners, his ghost searches for you on the road to Dartmouth.

II.

A thievery at Harvard University in 1833 resulted in a worldwide
search for Howard Jay. Found in Iowa—huffing over a hill—
by Don Bieber, a journalist, Jay addressed the thievery via song:
"Shun biography—just learn _is_ and _of_!"

Bieber shared the song with just six people: a jazz man, a critic,
a metamodernist author (Ronald Abramson), an editor,
a Dartmouth graduate (Ray Swensen), and a poet (Roger Trout).

And the attorney for Harvard—who shared it with the world.

III.

Born "Seth Abramson" in 1976, I can see that every word circles back:
Free. Abramson. Jazz.

A series of phrases, too: _Text not available. Net plus. The wide world._

Wide world is a lie. The world is only one spot in the universe. Just
one. A precise location. Ogle it and see which.

IV.

Every single video of a *suburb*—the net exclamation of silly Americans—
is *hypertext*. A collection of images. References. An ebb.

"Seth Abramson" is hypertext. One one six six eight three two zero zero
zero seconds. 396,000 "results." Plus a thousand poems composed
entirely of standard-issue ecstasies and phrases from the encyclopedia—
view these <u>here</u>.

Seth Abramson is *protocol*.

An Internet is more.

Additional feedback. More poems and results. More commercial phrases,
Twitter posts, literary contacts, and remixed poets. More Wisconsin, more
Iowa. More life.

Seth Abramson, use your posts to graduate—transfer—from Madison
to Google; from Google to Wikipedia; from Wikipedia
to "Seth Abramson"; from "Seth Abramson" to Seth Abramson.

"Point, click, follow—and 'Seth Abramson' is there." (Trademark!)

Seth Abramson: Commercial poet; catalog headshot; single yahoo
from Wisconsin; "post-poetry" author.

Commercial for Google.

Greatest Hits? "Writers' Workshop poet"; "Harvard Law poet"; "Dartmouth
College poet"; "Wisconsin-Madison poet"; "'Greatest Hits' feed"—Co-Editor
of *Best Experimental Three-Word Phrases*.

V.

Seth Abramson is one ton of secure commercial <u>hypertext</u>.

VI.

Seth Abramson is regarding Seth Abramson from the latest Omnidawn
catalog. "Check out Seth Abramson! Add Seth Abramson to Wikipedia!
Next, Google Seth Abramson! Contact Seth Abramson at school!
Post about Seth Abramson here! And 'relate' to Seth Abramson here!"

Go wide, Seth Abramson!

VII.

I point out Seth Abramson in Madison.

Seth Abramson, blogger. Seth Abramson, blog description.

Seth is *from* Madison; Seth is *of*
Twitter, Wikipedia, *Huffington Post* poems—"web poetry."

VIII.

"Who is Seth Abramson? Please share!"

Share news of? Privacy of? Poems of? Site organization of? Terms of?
Are works *wards*, born of education? Names? Age? Literary protocol?
Schools? Organizations? Ten thousand-ton critic-journalists? Email
lists? Feedback? Web commercials? Magazine links? Thirty Octobers
of "transfers"? Huffing? 1001000100101000100101001000?

IX.

Sixteenth Street. In the city. 1:01 pm. Barb Elliot is shopping.

(Buy Seth Abramson first!)

X.

Seth Abramson versus "Seth Abramson"!

Seth Abramson: Law school; blog editor; freelancer.
"Seth Abramson": Editor for Wesleyan!
Seth Abramson: Web poems.
"Seth Abramson": Web poems!
Seth Abramson: Words.
"Seth Abramson": Prize! Award! Seth Abramson's press!

XI.

Alphabetical key: Seth Abramson's 35+ arm!
                                   Seth Abramson's college!
                                   Seth Abramson's magazine!

XII.

In college, compose entirely freelance—entirely *secure*.
Compose poems because poems *learn*. Poems are like laws—
a secure foundation. Help edit "Seth Abramson," and
"Seth Abramson" may become free—"just" Seth Abramson.

[SEND.]

MORE WILL BE REVEALED LATER

I'm a multi-function device, my friend. Little rubber feet
laughing all over you. Features, attributes, benefits?
The most advanced yet accessible motherfucker lying in bed
and living on Lipitor. Lots of voluntary effort—
long on promises, short on delivery. I left a message
on your answering machine: "Learn once, repeat everywhere."

Mom, look what you started.

•

{evil grin}

•

Whatever you say—something sorry and straight, something
about a small, bald, unaudacious goal—learn your shit
or up and quit. Real-time is "somebody else's problem?"
Let me know how that works out for you. I know a lot of people
like that, and if you ask me, living large looks like trouble.

In other words: Do the right thing. Think globally, act locally.

•

"A work of art is a work in progress." Google that shit.

The ideal is intercourse and inebriation. I could be wrong.

Are you over eighteen? Are you in trouble? Smile
and read your friendly manual. (OK, read the *screen*, stupid.)
What you see looks pretty good
because the powers that be *want* to sell. Why? If I tell you,
will you buy me a drink?

I'm a subject-matter expert with a seriously impaired imagination—
"product superior to operator"—
a smart little rich kid skater smiling ear to ear, sitting in my chair
laughing (laughing to myself
with sugar, honey, and iced tea) and still in the dark about real life.

Real life is temporarily not available. Real life is career suicide.

Thank Science it's Friday. Until further notice, I'm taking a shower.
What's in it for me? Jerking off. Playing with myself.
Don't judge me: I search the web
and spank the monkey. A single point of contact *works* for me.

Short on time? This says it all: "Life's fucked up—there's a hole
in the middle of the sea. Without a doubt,
everyone is laughing *at* you or laughing *about* you. Keep calm
and carry on."

·

In search of ecstasy? Let it go! Ecstasy is weather without the wait.

·

Change of subject: You wish I was you, clad in naught by air.
Unpleasant visual! Trust me, you'd hate to be me: toes up, tired,
shaking my head, short on time, trying to keep a straight face.
(The list goes on.) That's life in the big city. Traffic, titty bars,
terms and conditions, single white females, soon-to-be exes,
sexually transmitted diseases,
standing room only, sensitive New Age guys, "not safe for work",
quality control, "this job beats no job", thanks "in advance",
"tall, dark, and handsome", "try before you buy". In other words,
player versus player. Sit and sweat.
Same shit, different day. And the end of the world as we know it.

Sleepy city, better you than me.

•

New college graduate? Double incomes, no kids? Single income,
two children, oppressive mortgage? What the Hell is next? What's
in it for you? You never know. And do I look like I give a shit?

(Wouldn't it be nice if well-off older folks—very sad faces!—
picked up Ecstasy? "Why should I wait? The sooner, the better!")

•

Teachers are watching. (Side note: Who cares? There ain't no justice.)

"Please turn off your electronic devices!" She who must be obeyed,
screaming with laughter—there ought to be a law—rings my bell.

Roundhouse kick!

(Rank has its privileges. The rest are mine.)

"Point of view is a personal problem." Piss off! So I see rainbows, butterflies, and unicorns—to be honest, what's the difference between rainbows, butterflies, and unicorns?

(You tell me, parent over shoulder, person of no account!)

•

{away from keyboard}

•

People like us press lots of keys to abort. Quick question: Why should I wait? Fear of getting caught? Something like that?

Male or female, you always have options: north, east, west, south.

"You talk too much—without thinking too much."

You know what? You don't know me, old man.

•

You may already know: Portland is generally recognized as safe. In other words, on the road or out to lunch, get off the damn phone while you're driving. Overcome by events? A person in need? Hitting bottom and starting to dig? First Lady of the United States? Get off the damn phone while you're driving.

Don't ask me how I know that.

•

Quoted for truth in your fucking dreams—good for one night—
"Obligatory energy is the enemy." Obligatory energy
is not too bright—out of touch—and not invented here (Portland).

Not interested. Not in *this* lifetime!

•

Tomorrow is cancelled. Owing to a slight oversight in construction—
a process too complicated to explain—
I just ejaculated on my keyboard.

My kind of place.

A BUG DIES (AND ON ITS BACKSIDE, TOO)

What does my face look like
when pity wobbles up in stalagmites?
I become the garish sparkle of morning,
rotting in ecstasy. Terrible and sudden—
a Greek. (In my eye sockets are words
grazing the floor, orchestrating.)

Your face looks no longer. Should I
be concerned? With God quiet,
watch when adults play games—
there are no stakes. "With God,"
the poster says, "I closed every gate."

•

When I laugh, I'd like you behind me.

•

We walk to the park with our beliefs.
We are sad. And this means the Net emoji
all day show my true leanings.

Why, when we stand next to the facts,
our supper is cold and flat! The bed creaks!
A mitten falls on its back! I could cry.

From my bedroom—and my drunk
particles on your apartment ceiling—
what I say is: "Full faces are sexy!
Break my heart some other way!"

•

My daughter's name is Frances,
and she is buried. Neighbor, would "never"
wake her pink arm?
The myth of a sparrow in a bucket?
The mountains of Colorado? Canada?

Bees? Wii? Trade? A canoe?

(When one falls from the gauze, it turns.
Does so much fall down?)

•

Sword? Bow? No longer.

Concerned to imagine me sleeping
in the motorcycle cafe? My flowered tights?

•

I lick.

I sing.

From me—lonely, stringing—to her, golden.

•

We never looked up.

TAYLOR SWIFT: GREATEST HITS, VOL. 1

(four-word phrases from every song by Taylor Swift,
arranged in the order the songs were released)

On back roads at night, never let me drive. I can't even see
what's down this road.

Every smile you faked, I went looking for.
Don't tell anyone that. It's like the radio—
a moment of weakness bigger than me.

You turn the radio down, listen to the crickets.
You stop and stare, tear it all apart
with tired eyes. I mention one little thing: pure light.
Radiant beams in a cardboard box.

I used to know people, say things. I can't tell you why
we almost never speak,
because I'm too tired and everyone knows who I really want.
Is the pavement you walk who you're gonna be?
See the lights, see 50 reasons why I honestly believed in you.

When you wake up, I see your face, bulletproof. But I'm not.

•

Pick up the phone and it's 2AM and a Tuesday.

When I found a town "far in," and we sang, you saw me start
like a full-on rainstorm,
work and the weather rudely barging in.

On your long list of words—like "knives" and "swords"—
the story of us could still be simple, like passing notes
in prep school.

So it shattered on the floor.

To see it break, to feel you breathe—the cynics were outraged.
Time's theirs, seems like.

Come back to me, or go to work changing minds.

We fall down a dead-end street, out of focus.
I knew you were trouble, but something about it
was miserable and magical.

This time of night, I used to think I love you.
Because the last time I had something to lose—
sad, beautiful, tragic love—I showed up here.

You held the door.

We were dancing, on a Wednesday, in the bathroom.

·

I try falling in love in what's upstanding and right—
the way *you* love what you're doing.

Right in the palm of an American boy,
American girl—raised on promises—I'd rather you be looking
through *your* eyes, wondering where we are
until you come up, come to my door, and lay down your guns.

My whole damn life, I'd have never guessed this time
would come. Don't need the *real*—there's so much more.

.

In dark blue Tennessee, she walks to school,
finally eye to eye with drops of Jupiter.
(Every lesson forms a line. Cross it out—you were meant to.)
She's finally well enough to talk about why
the saddest fear comes on a plane—
and that passenger seat has unfamiliar exit signs.

I spent a long time in this little town.

I would've stayed, but I'm not gonna.

I know the mistake I can't confess
was waiting there for you. It hits me, then: I still love you.
Could've spent a life cleaning up that mess,
but I'm dressed to remember your bare feet, your eyes,
the sun, a piece of driftwood spinning around...

I'm spinning.

(Stupid boy!)

I've been laying in the green life, sweeter than fiction.
What it cost me? It's all the rage:
true love. Should've tangled like the roots I dreamed about.

Rapping made sense until the morning.

•

I sleep alone, scared of the world. I hate those voices
my imagination is running. The moment's getting nearer

I want to talk about you. And if you lie awake at night, I
turn around.

JUSTIN BIEBER: GREATEST HITS, VOL. 1

(four-word phrases from every song by Justin Bieber,
arranged in the order the songs were released)

My fight is your fairytale
and show. Them walking in the dark believe me.

Like a fourteenth of February, not dancing close—
I'm telling you—with me, girl, changed the game.
      Now, *un peu plus fort*, I'm going down.

Down I bring the sun—it's reckless and clumsy—
and all it offers my baby over here is *love*.
Let the back and forth that wind (wind! wind! wind!)
is easy to
      get harder to shield.

This is a definite possibility when you're not with me.

Down I will fight for love (or somebody to love).
I can make the gray pull me up, I can live it up
deep inside me.

There, everything I wished for in the winter snow
will find it hard.

•

You better watch out. When the lights go,
      there upon the fireplace I might go psycho.

(Nobody can see me watching the snow fall,
looking out the window so tender and mild.)

Baby, I will not cry when your heart beats—
I lose my appetite for you and me when people say
you could be my girlfriend
as long as you have a reputation. Oh baby, I'm here
but enough is enough.

I'll catch you, as much as I don't know how.

•

It's beauty from the streets I want.

I know across the ocean, across how I got here,
you're the only one getting to the point. (*I never hit it.*)

Let me ask you, what's on your mind
when you love me and you miss me
but I know about seven billion people in the world?

We're young. Don't like this life? Let's start tonight:
You forget the way you want to be loved—
        all the way around—
and I'm sure that anytime you ask me what we had,
I'll pick up your presence. It feels like a wristwatch,
so hard
        nothing else really matters.

•

Life's so unpredictable! Your worst enemy, sometimes.
But the best. So come and go, baby,
accept all the responsibility. Dance with the money,
it may be different when the rhythm's on.

We just need forgiveness, over and over again.

24/7.

Every single time love was interrupted by Facebook.

.

All the time I was your boyfriend, I knew you were wishing
you could be home, where you belong.

(Every city and every country you don't know,
I'm starting to like.)

I don't *need* music; I could get over it. It's hard,
not beautiful.

I've never seen you *believe*. (Believe! Believe!)
Don't run off and dance under the sky!
People in their basements might as well just wipe away
their memory!

(That makes you laugh? .... I really like you.)

You and I make the highest point—yes! And I know
I want you.
So, forget all the guys—this is Justin, thinking about you.

And forced to change.

Your head on my shoulder in the moonlight: I smile,
for a minute.

BEST ALBUMS OF 2013: #34

      Lines curl ominously, warning. Shadows debut, life-sized.
Hypnotizing pipes, carving out a fully inhabitable world, power
the future. Like timeless engravings of _____ at _____.

E.P. Leone, yawning in shades—
fertile, a producer—is observing it all. His guitar occupies time.

(The soundtrack will one day matter. Drums have boundaries.)

No one excels at atmosphere like Leone. His predecessor, a bum,
nameless, scrabbles between slippery feelings. The eastern folk
call out to the western in celebration, and the listener is forgotten—
like words to forests, offhand swords.

A slow and steady dagger in a Manchester forest. Such engravings
on it! The heart of the forest is interested in telling a story: "Swords
      triumph, not memories!"
Engravings promise music to our children's children—and doom.

All paths criss-cross in the next, nameless territory.

Music: one minute evoking, the next placeless and undefinable.
An album feels deeply meaningful, and yet it rejects—again—
the subconscious. (Like engravings from—*of*—2010.)
And yet, what seems like early fluidity is instead an unmaking.

Throughout the earth are
sounds (the unquestionable part of manner): "Buy this! And that!"

      The chasm fulfills, in its way. It does. But.

III

T.C. BOYLE, "ON SO-CALLED 'METAMODERNISM'"

A student (I won't use her real name) came to my office one Tuesday for a regularly scheduled appointment. Even after having taught for so many years, I felt a little anxious about this particular meeting, the reason being that this student had just handed in what I considered a very disappointing piece of work. It was poetry, too, which obviously isn't my "home genre"—though I certainly know enough. Even now I'd be hard-pressed to describe exactly what this student had produced, except to say that I disliked it intensely. The language was glossy and insubstantial in the same way the nightly news is, or I guess maybe the nightly news if you get it online rather than through one of the major broadcast or cable networks. And there was no sense of distance whatsoever between the author and the text, as though the poetry were processing information being fed to its author in real time. Obviously I've seen this sort of thing before; anyone who's taught creative writing to undergraduates has. But it's usually a poem

{violin}

about some concert the student attended, or an art show, or a fraternity or sorority party, or a family trip, or whatever. This wasn't anything like that, and the language wasn't anything like you'd expect in a poem that merely reproduces an experience immediately after the fact. The language felt oddly constrained, in the sense that it felt both natural and unnatural at the same time. At ease with itself and decidedly not. There were some very good parts, I suppose, but then also some very bad ones, which of course always calls into question whether the good parts were merely fortuitous— as we can safely assume the bad ones were accidental. And the tone was indecipherable.

I sensed that this student (let's call her "Sheila") had been consuming some sort of traumatic language recently, and instead of getting the time and distance from a trauma we always think of as essential to both poetry and fiction, instead of taking the time to get anything *right*, she'd decided to do away with the longstanding dichotomy between the language of art and the language of information and assemble this unholy hodgepodge of the two. Which meant there were moments of elevated language sitting alongside some really sloppy, loose talk about abstract ideas; prosaic language alongside obviously concept-driven blips and beeps; a clear narrative coupled with textual chaos that was nearly impossible to process or take seriously. Parts of it were actually—I don't know if this is really the word I want, but here it is—

irresponsible. There was angry speech alongside anxiously compassionate lines; phrases that were discernibly childish leading into languid, nearly Romantic ones that ticked several of the boxes we associate with immaculate craft. I mean it was just all over the place: sincere then ironic, idealistic then cynical, organic then inorganic, epic then anecdotal. So I wasn't looking forward to talking with Sheila because what am I going to say? This is a mess and needs to be tossed? You're really not justifying your teaching assistantship? I question your motives? You're not putting the sort of careful pressure on language we'd expect from a professional artist?

{violin}{snare}

I heard her coming down the hallway before I heard the knock on my office door, which I remember only because it's an odd thing to remember and not something I normally would. If I had to say, I'd say—I guess—that she was "walking heavy." And when I opened the door to invite her inside she *looked* heavy, too. I mean, like, in the spiritual sense. Something was weighing heavily on her. So I thought to myself that this conference already had a ready opening, given as how, you know, she clearly wanted to unburden herself, which was fine by me, both because I didn't know yet what I was going to say to her and because this had historically been, like, a pretty strong student—one of my best, really—so I figured she had the chops to lead our conversation down the road it needed to go.

{violin}{snare}{cymbal}

So this is what Shelly said to me, and of course I'm paraphrasing. She didn't say exactly this, and she didn't say it as well as I'll say it now, but the ideas were there and with some time and reflection (and an hour on Google) I've been able to connect the dots well enough, I think. So, like, this is what she said: "Professor Boyle, I know what I handed in looks like a mess. I think it's because, like, my head is a little bit messy right now. Not, you know, emotionally—I mean about my writing. Alice [this is another student and another nom de plume here] and I were talking about some things after class last week and she told me that she'd read a paper from the David Foster Wallace conference in New Mexico last year. Someone there was calling Wallace a 'metamodern' writer. So Alice thought, you know, why don't we look this up online? Because she really likes DFW. Especially his essays. I wasn't very interested because I don't believe in '-isms,' because fiction really isn't my home genre though I know it well enough, because I don't like theory or whatever, and because I really didn't come here to get 'academic' about my poetry or talk about 'poetics' or whatever, just to figure out how to write well. But then it felt like Alice was making some interesting points about, you know, Art, and, I don't know. I felt like Alice had been walking pretty heavy for a while—does that make sense?—so I was inclined to hear her out. Which I did. And then a lot of things got pretty muddled for me."

{violin}{snare}{cymbal}
{violin}{snare}{cymbal}
{violin}{snare}{cymbal}{flute}
{violin}{snare}{cymbal}

This is where a better professor would have interjected in some way to direct the discussion. Asked questions, maybe dropped some passive-aggressive hint—"I've never heard the term 'metamodern' before, Cynthia, so..."—as a way of steering the conversation back to anything productive. But it was a Tuesday, and I'm not much on Tuesdays. So I just told her to go on. And she said something like (same apologies as above) this: "Alice was asking why poems need to have a consistent tone? She was asking, like, why we need to have this distance or whatever from whatever we write? Why can't a line just be bad—by design—not to be funny or expose the infirmities of language or whatever but because sometimes poets are bad at what they do, and sometimes humans are bad at being human, and sometimes you want to leave a reader guessing about what was intentional and what wasn't, what could be helped and what couldn't be? Why can't the fact that we've come through seventy years of postmodernism still wanting to feel *human*, still *wanting* despite all we've learned, show up as an earnest badness or other kind of tasteless transgression in the work? Why [and here she used Robert Frost as an example] can't we write things that scare people, or make people angry, or that are [though she probably didn't put it this way] dishonest?" "'Dishonest' how?" I asked her, fixing my attention on that word in particular. "Well, okay, why can't you, you know, try to convince people, in really clear and transparent language, of a lie? Given that that's the sort of experience we all have when we watch television, movies, Internet porn, everything? Why can't a poem exhibit the same lack of focus social media does? The same plasticity, coupled with an occasional solemnity and even profundity? Why can't we misappropriate language instead of appropriating it? Reappropriate it instead of transcribing it? Mistranscribe it instead of juxtaposing it? Unjuxtapose it but keep it emotionally unprocessable? Process it instead of crafting or interpreting it? Why can't you try to *unsettle* readers somehow? Have an effect? Have that effect be ambiguous? Not just ventriloquize but write *as*, say, anything or anyone, like John Cusack or James Franco? Be both conceptual and confessional? Both sharp and slack? And Alice was saying also that she couldn't see why writing in the first person was so bad if you could find a way to get enough distance from yourself that every time you used 'I' it was sort of you, sort of someone else, sort of everyone, sort of no one, sort of a comment on how everyone's personal mythos has somehow survived postmodernism." So here's where I stepped in

{violin}{snare}{cymbal}
{violin}{snare}{cymbal}
{violin}{snare}{cymbal}{flute}
{violin}{snare}{cymbal}{bassoon}
{violin}{snare}{cymbal}{bassoon}{chimes}
{violin}{snare}{cymbal}{bassoon}
{violin}{snare}{cymbal}{flute}
{violin}{snare}{cymbal}{bassoon}
{violin}{snare}{cymbal}{bassoon}{chimes}
{violin}{snare}{cymbal}{bassoon}
{violin}{snare}{cymbal}{flute}
{violin}{snare}{cymbal}

and said that of course you can do all these things, but one doesn't need to slap a label on it to make it more important than it is. And I added that the final determination of any strategy one uses in writing a poem is whether the poem places pressure on language in an interesting way, and does so with a level of care we'd associate with advanced compositional techniques. I mentioned also that putting labels on one's own writing as part of developing a "poetics" or whatever just isn't done—that's what scholars are for, you know, and that's why artists wait for scholars to talk about them instead of talking about (or even among) themselves about the sorts of things Alice was so preoccupied with. And here's where Lila got animated, and I'm really going to start summarizing in my own words because what she said didn't make any sense. She said

{violin}{snare}{cymbal}
{violin}{cello}{snare}{cymbal}
{violin}{cello}{snare}{cymbal}{flute}

{violin}{cello}{snare}{cymbal}{bassoon}
{violin}{cello}{snare}{cymbal}{bassoon}{chimes}
{violin}{cello}{snare}{cymbal}{contrabassoon}
{violin}{cello}{snare}{cymbal}{flute}
{violin}{cello}{snare}{cymbal}{bassoon}
{violin}{cello}{snare}{cymbal}{bassoon}{chimes}
{violin}{cello}{snare}{cymbal}{contrabassoon}
{violin}{cello}{snare}{cymbal}{flute}
{violin}{cello}{snare}{cymbal}
{snare}{cello}
{snare}{cello}
{violin}{snare}{cymbal}
{violin}{cello}{snare}{cymbal}
{violin}{cello}{snare}{cymbal}{flute}
{violin}{cello}{snare}{cymbal}{bassoon}
{violin}{cello}{snare}{cymbal}{bassoon}{chimes}
{violin}{cello}{snare}{cymbal}{contrabassoon}
{violin}{cello}{snare}{cymbal}{flute}
{violin}{cello}{snare}{cymbal}{bassoon}
{violin}{cello}{snare}{cymbal}{bassoon}{chimes}
{violin}{cello}{snare}{cymbal}{contrabassoon}
{violin}{cello}{snare}{cymbal}{flute}
{violin}{cello}{snare}{cymbal}

that what I was describing to her—care; attention; craft; distance; consistency; the calibration of intent but not response; letting language units be the primary unit of measure in language—sounds absolutely nothing like the Internet, or 4chan, or a thousand channels of cable, and as she and her generation have been raised as much by the Internet and cable as anything or anyone else, why should either her mode of composition or the composition itself conform to an understanding of Art that was miles away from her experience of life, and more suitable to her parent's pre-Internet, six-channel generation than her own? Why did poetry have to feel so distant all the time, when every other stimulant in her life was pounding pounding pounding in her brain all hours of the day? She loves poetry, she loves poetry more than anything else, she's willing to lose everything for Art, so why when something important happens to me or my friends or my community am I supposed to take a few weeks to draft a perfectly appropriate response in line with approved modern or postmodern writing techniques, all the while further ensuring that I'm doing my small part to keep poetry on the perimeter of American life? Why can't my compositional method be synchronous with the sociocultural framework of the Age? Why can't I risk a blindingly fast oscillation between—or even a sublime juxtaposition of—sloppiness and mastery, or caution and recklessness, when the present state of the species and my life is exactly this? Why can't I acknowledge that things fall apart but nevertheless seek to advance a claim of subjectivity and even goddammit hope I know is always-already compromised? Why can't I choose ambiguous transcendence over the banality of obvious craft? Why don't creative writing programs teach poets how to go on the Internet and do something other than offer up affective responses, ad hominem attacks, and by-the-book craft readings of work that makes them uncomfortable or offends their received sensibilities, when we'd discourage such intellectual mayonnaise from even the first-semester freshmen here at UW-Madison? Why can't poetry be a critical and communal data-processing praxis capable of reifying everything I actually know or think I should know, everything I actually feel or think I should feel, and everything I experience but can't process properly or responsibly, both the naive and idealistic ambitions of modernism and the cynical refusals of postmodernism, expressing not my fear of how the generations that preceded mine will receive my work, expressing not the craven zeitgeist of our literary moment, but above all the state of suspended confusion MY WHOLE FUCKING GEN

{808}{violin}{snare}{cymbal}
{808}{violin}{cello}{snare}{cymbal}
{808}{violin}{cello}{snare}{cymbal}{flute}
{808}{violin}{cello}{snare}{cymbal}{bassoon}
{808}{violin}{cello}{snare}{cymbal}{bassoon}{chimes}
{808}{violin}{cello}{snare}{cymbal}{contrabassoon}
{808}{violin}{cello}{snare}{cymbal}{flute}
{808}{violin}{cello}{snare}{cymbal}{bassoon}
{808}{violin}{cello}{snare}{cymbal}{bassoon}{chimes}
{808}{violin}{cello}{snare}{cymbal}{contrabassoon}
{808}{violin}{cello}{snare}{cymbal}{flute}
{808}{violin}{cello}{snare}{cymbal}
{808}{snare}{cello}
{808}{snare}{cello}

{oboe}{clarinet}{french horn}

{808}

{oboe}{clarinet}{french horn}

{808}

{oboe}{clarinet}{french horn}

{808}

{oboe}{clarinet}{french horn}

{808}

{oboe}{clarinet}{french horn}

{808}

{808}{violin}{snare}{cymbal}

{808}{violin}{cello}{snare}{cymbal}

{808}{violin}{cello}{snare}{cymbal}{flute}{clarinet}{french horn}

{808}{violin}{cello}{snare}{cymbal}{bassoon}{clarinet}{french horn}

{808}{violin}{cello}{snare}{cymbal}{bassoon}{chimes}

{808}{violin}{cello}{snare}{cymbal}{contrabassoon}

{808}{violin}{cello}{snare}{cymbal}{flute}{clarinet}{french horn}

{808}{violin}{cello}{snare}{cymbal}{bassoon}{clarinet}{french horn}

{808}{violin}{cello}{snare}{cymbal}{bassoon}{chimes}

{808}{violin}{cello}{snare}{cymbal}{contrabassoon}

{808}{violin}{cello}{snare}{cymbal}{flute}{clarinet}{french horn}

{808}{violin}{cello}{snare}{cymbal}

{808}{violin}{snare}{cymbal}

{808}respect the fact that many have thought very hard

{808}{violin}{cello}{snare}{cymbal}

{808}{violin}{cello}{snare}{cymbal}{flute}

{808}{violin}{cello}{snare}{cymbal}{bassoon}

{808}{violin}{cello}{snare}{cymbal}{bassoon}{chimes}

{808}{violin}{cello}{snare}{cymbal}{contrabassoon}

{808}{violin}{cello}every student thinks they can{snare}{cymbal}{flute}

{808}{violin}{cello}{snare}{cymbal}{bassoon}

{808}{violin}{cello}{snare}{cymbal}{bassoon}{chimes}

{808}{violin}{cello}something "new"{snare}{cymbal}{contrabassoon}

{808}{violin}{cello}{snare}{cymbal}{flute}

{808}{violin}{cello}{snare}{cymbal}

{808}{snare}{cello}

{808}{snare}poetry can deliver a counterpoint to this wasteful haste{cello} {oboe}{clarinet}{french horn}

{808}{double bass}

{oboe}{clarinet}{french horn}{double bass}

{808}{double bass}

{oboe}{clarinet}{french horn}{double bass}

{808}{double bass}

{oboe}{clarinet}{french horn}{double bass}

{808}{double bass}

{oboe}{clarinet}{french horn}{double bass}

{808}{double bass}

{808}{violin}{snare}{cymbal}{double bass}

{808}{violin}{cello}{snare}{cymbal}{double bass}

{808}{violin}{cello}{snare}{cymbal}{flute}{double bass}

{808}{violin}{cello}{snare}{cymbal}{bassoon}{double bass}

{808}{violin}{cello}{snare}{cymbal}{bassoon}{chimes}{double bass}

{808}{violin}{cello}{snare}should calm down and stop thinking that{cymbal}{bassoon}

{808}{violin}{cello}{snare}{cymbal}{flute}{double bass}

{808}{violin}{cello}{snare}{cymbal}{bassoon}{double bass}

{808}{violin}{cello}{snare}{cymbal}{bassoon}{chimes}{double bass}

{808}{violin}{cello}{snare}{cymbal}{contrabassoon}{double bass}

{808}{violin}{cello}difficult for a man to have a stake{snare}{cymbal}{flute}{double bass}

{808}{violin}{cello}{snare}{cymbal}{double bass}

{violin}{cello}{snare}{cymbal}

{808}

{808}

{808}

{808}

{808}

{808}

{808}

{808}

{808}

a place of privilege

{808}

{808}

{808}

{808}

{808}

{808}

{808}

{808}

{808}

{808}

{808}{violin}

{808}{violin}

{808}{violin}

{808}{violin}

{808}{violin}

{808}{violin}{cello}

{808}{violin}or wise up{cello}

{808}{violin}{cello}

{808}{violin}{cello}

{808}{violin}{cello}

{808}{violin}{cello}{full kit}

{808}{violin}{cello}{full kit}

{808}{violin}{cello}{full kit}

{808}{violin}{cello}{full kit}

{808}{violin}{cello}{full kit}

{808}{violin}{cello}{full kit}{flute}

{808}{violin}{cello}{full kit}{flute}

{808}{violin}{cello}{full kit}{flute}

{808}{violin}{cello}{full kit}{flute}

{808}{violin}{cello}{full kit}{flute}

{808}{violin}{cello}{full kit}{flute}{double bass}

{808}{violin}{cello}{full kit}{flute}{double bass}

{808}{violin}{cello}{full kit}{flute}{double bass}

{808}{violin}{cello}{full kit}{flute}{double bass}

{808}{violin}{cello}{full kit}{flute}{double bass}

{808}{violin}{cello}{full kit}{flute}{double bass}{tuba}

{808}{violin}{cello}{full kit}{flute}{double bass}{tuba}

{808}{violin}{cello}{full kit}{flute}{double bass}{tuba}

{808}{violin}{cello}{full kit}{flute}{double bass}{tuba}

{808}{violin}{cello}{full kit}{flute}{double bass}{tuba}
{808}{violin}{cello}{full kit}{flute}{double bass}{tuba}
{808}{violin}{cello}{full kit}{flute}{double bass}{tuba}
{808}{violin}{cello}{full kit}{flute}{double bass}{tuba}
{808}{violin}{cello}{full kit}{flute}{double bass}{tuba}
{808}{violin}{cello}{full kit}{flute}{double bass}{tuba}
{808}{violin}{cello}{full kit}{flute}{double bass}{tuba}
{808}
{808}
{808}
{808}
{808}

REALITY IS A UNIT OF MEASURE

{8o{violin}8}
{8o{violin}8}
{8o{violin}8}
{8o{violin}8}
{8o{violin}8}
{8o{violin}8}{vio{cello}lin}
{8o{violin}8}{vio{cello}lin}
{8o{violin}8}{vio{cello}lin}
{8o{violin}8}{vio{cello}lin}
{8o{violin}8}{vio{cello}lin}
{8o{violin}8}{vio{cello}lin}{cel{full kit}lo}
{8o{violin}8}{vio{cello}lin}{cel{full kit}lo}
{8o{violin}8}{vio{cello}lin}{cel{full kit}lo}
{8o{violin}8}{vio{cello}lin}{cel{full kit}lo}
{8o{violin}8}{vio{cello}lin}{cel{full kit}lo}
{8o{violin}8}{vio{cello}lin}{cello}{full{flute} kit}
{8o{violin}8}{vio{cello}lin}{cello}{full{flute} kit}
{8o{violin}8}{vio{cello}lin}{cello}{full{flute} kit}
{8o{violin}8}{vio{cello}lin}{cello}{full{flute} kit}
{8o{violin}8}{vio{cello}lin}{cello}{full{flute} kit}
{8o{violin}8}{vio{cello}lin}{cello}{full kit}{flu{double bass}te}
{8o{violin}8}{vio{cello}lin}{cello}{full kit}{flu{double bass}te}
{8o{violin}8}{vio{cello}lin}{cello}{full kit}{flu{double bass}te}
{8o{violin}8}{vio{cello}lin}{cello}{full kit}{flu{double bass}te}

{80{violin}8}{vio{cello}lin}{cello}{full kit}{flu{double bass}te}
{80{violin}8}{vio{cello}lin}{cello}{full kit}{flute}{dou{tuba}ble bass}
{80{violin}8}{vio{cello}lin}{cello}{full kit}{flute}{dou{tuba}ble bass}
{80{violin}8}{vio{cello}lin}{cello}{full kit}{flute}{dou{tuba}ble bass}
{80{violin}8}{vio{cello}lin}{cello}{full kit}{flute}{dou{tuba}ble bass}
{80{violin}8}{vio{cello}lin}{cello}{full kit}{flute}{dou{tuba}ble bass}
{80{violin}8}{vio{cello}lin}{cello}{full kit}{flute}{double bass}{tuba}
{80{violin}8}{vio{cello}lin}{cello}{full kit}{flute}{double bass}{tu{808}ba}
{80{violin}8}{vio{cello}lin}{cello}{full kit}{flute}{double bass}{tu{808}ba}
{80{violin}8}{vio{cello}lin}{cello}{full kit}{flute}{double bass}{tu{808}ba}
{80{violin}8}{vio{cello}lin}{cello}{full kit}{flute}{double bass}{tu{808}ba}
{80{violin}8}{vio{cello}lin}{cello}{full kit}{flute}{double bass}{tuba}{80{808}8}
{80{violin}8}{vio{cello}lin}{cello}{full kit}{flute}{double bass}{tuba}{80{808}8}
{80{violin}8}{vio{cello}lin}{cello}{full kit}{flute}{double bass}{tuba}{80{808}8}
{80{violin}8}{vio{cello}lin}{cello}{full kit}{flute}{double bass}{tuba}{80{808}8}
{80{violin}8}{vio{cello}lin}{cello}{full kit}{flute}{double bass}{tuba}{80{808}8}
{80{violin}8}{vio{cello}lin}{cello}{full kit}{flute}{double bass}{tuba}{80{808}8}
{80{violin}8}{vio{cello}lin}{cello}{full kit}{flute}{double bass}{tuba}{808}
{80{violin}8}{vio{cello}lin}{cello}{full kit}{flute}{double bass}{tuba}
{80{violin}8}{vio{cello}lin}{cello}{full kit}{flute}{double bass}
{80{violin}8}{vio{cello}lin}{cello}{full kit}{flute}
{80{violin}8}{vio{cello}lin}{cello}{full kit}
{80{violin}8}{vio{cello}lin}{cello}
{80{violin}8}{vio{cello}lin}
{80{violin}8}
{808}
{808}
{808}
{808}
{808}
{808}
{808}
{808}
{808}
Life has attracted me, life has denied me; forced me to give, forced me to take; spoiled me, tried me, hit me; desired me like a girlfriend, treated me like a sex crime. I will never give up. I will never be stuck *inside* life. I deserve better

{808}

{808}

{808}

{808}

{808}

I

{808}

{808}

{808}

{808}

{808}

I

{808}

I

{808}

I

{808}

I

{808}

I

{808}

I

{808}

I

{808}

I

{808}

I

{808}

I

{808}

{I}

{808}

{I}

{808}

{I}

{808}

{I}

{808}

{I}

{808}

{I}

{808}

{I}

{808}

{I}

{I}{808}{violin}{cello}

{I}{808}{violin}{cello}

{I}{808}{violin}{cello}

{I}{808}{violin}{cello}

{I}{808}{violin}{cello}

{I}{808}{violin}{cello}{full kit}

{I}{808}{violin}{cello}{full kit}

{I}{808}{violin}{cello}{full kit}

{I}{808}{violin}{cello}{full kit}

{I}{808}{violin}{cello}{full kit}

{I}{808}{violin}{cello}{full kit}{flute}

{I}{808}{violin}{cello}{full kit}{flute}

{I}{808}{violin}{cello}{full kit}{flute}

{I}{808}{violin}{cello}{full kit}{flute}

{I}{808}{violin}{cello}{full kit}{flute}

{I}{808}{violin}{cello}{full kit}{flute}{double bass}

{I}{808}{violin}{cello}{full kit}{flute}{double bass}

{I}{808}{violin}{cello}{full kit}{flute}{double bass}

{I}{808}{violin}{cello}{full kit}{flute}{double bass}

{I}{808}{violin}{cello}{full kit}{flute}{double bass}

{I}{808}{violin}{cello}{full kit}{flute}{double bass}{tuba}

{I}{808}{violin}{cello}{full kit}{flute}{double bass}{tuba}{car}{click}{beep}{ring}{click}

{I}{violin}{cello}{full kit}{flute}{double bass}{tuba}{car}{click}{beep}{ring}{click}

{I}{cello}{full kit}{flute}{double bass}{tuba}{car}{click}{beep}{ring}{click}

{I}{full kit}{flute}{double bass}{tuba}{car}{click}{beep}{ring}{click}

{I}{flute}{double bass}{tuba}{car}{click}{beep}{ring}{click}

{I}{double bass}{tuba}{car}{click}{beep}{ring}{click}
{I}{tuba}{car}{click}{beep}{ring}{click}
{I}{car}{click}{beep}{ring}{click}
{I}{click}{beep}{ring}{click}
{I}{beep}{ring}{click}
{I}{ring}{click}
{I}{click}
{I}{click}
{I}{click}
{I}{click}
{I}{click}
{I}{click}
{I}{click}
{I}{click}
{I}
{click)

I

IV

CLICKBAIT #1

"Reading Rainbow" finishes Kickstarter campaign strong with $5.4 million

Keith Wagstaff, NBC News

Like a butterfly in the sky, the "Reading Rainbow" Kickstarter project went five times as high as its original goal, raising $5.4 million when the campaign officially ended on Wednesday night. It turns out that a catchy theme song, nostalgia, and promoting children's literacy is a recipe for success: The crowdfunding campaign hit its original goal, $1 million, in only 11 hours, and went on to become the most-backed Kickstarter project in history.

Not only that, but the project also raised serious cash from "Family Guy" creator Seth MacFarlane, who pledged to match every dollar up to $1 million—provided donors passed the $4 million mark. They did, and the project to bring "Reading Rainbow" to the Web, smartphones, and game consoles ended up raising a total of more than $6.4 million. LeVar Burton has yet to release a teary "thank you" video to fans, but he did share the news on Twitter: http://www.twitter.com/levarburton.

Two retired Mexican infantrymen, both veterans of the U.S.-Mexican War—a conflict that lasted from 1846 to 1848—remain inseparable friends after their unit disbands. The two spend most days reminiscing about Resaca de la Palma, a battle fought on May 9th, 1846 on the banks of the Rio Grande. There, U.S. General (later 12th U.S. President) Zachary Taylor routed regiments under the command of General Mariano Arista. Among the regiments under Arista's command was the 7th Mexican Infantry, for which detachment the former infantrymen now discussed both fought.

On the Mexican side, the result of Resaca de la Palma was 515 killed, wounded, or missing. Arista's men managed to kill 33 Americans and critically injure 89 others. The first of the two aging Mexican veterans, Hernandez, personally killed 3 Americans and wounded 2 in the battle; his friend, Fernando, killed 5 and wounded 3. It's these 8 kills and 5 serious injuries that the two celebrate near-daily as they sit in creaky chairs at a nursing home in San Juan Bautista. Hernandez in particular has vivid memories of the 7th Infantry crossing the Rio Grande to meet Taylor's advancing 3rd, 4th, and 5th foot regiments and a squadron of skirmishers led by Captain William W. Mackall. He recalls that May 9th, 1846 was a clear night, and that Arista's men—all of whom earnestly believed themselves freedom fighters—were certain they'd defeat the force massing before them. The belief was not unreasonable, given their numbers, training, and equipment. And yet, while Arista had 4,000 men to Taylor's 1,700, the former's troops (including both Hernandez and Fernando) were mostly young and untested.

On one particular day in 1903, the now 73-year-old Hernandez and now 76-year-old Fernando are sitting in the day room at La Hacienda in San Juan Bautista speaking, once again, of Resaca de la Palma. (Well, Hernandez is speaking, as by now Fernando has ceased communicating altogether.) Hernandez reads his old comrade's reactions by watching the other man's slowly dimming gray-blue eyes. Hernandez recalls how Fernando played his *vihuela* (a guitar-like stringed instrument) before the battle; concedes that he quivered with fear at the approach of the Americans' 3rd foot; and regales Fernando with a vivid portrait of the hundreds of Mexican and American corpses that littered the shores of the Rio Grande after the battle. Hernandez speaks with particular delight, and in unusually grisly detail, of the 3 Americans he killed that night. After describing to Fernando his final kill of the battle—the strangulation ("With a half rotted canteen strap, Fernando!") of a 13 year-old drummer boy—he remarks, with barely concealed fervor, "And if I had to do the same again, I *would*." His eyes mist as he hears once more the death rattle of that little gringo cocksucker.

Sometimes, friends, war is beautiful.

HIT IT!

http://www.youtube.com/watch?v=dQsjAbZDx-4

A young woman has spent the last year in an abusive relationship. As in many such situations, certain markers are present: the couple routinely ends, then restarts their relationship; the man promises to change his behavior, but these promises rarely last a week; and hateful words are exchanged that open wounds which will never heal.

This particular young woman has had it especially hard. Her boyfriend, Jake, abandons her for weeks at a time, only to outrageously claim, on his return, that she's crowding him and he "needs more space." His fervent promises to cease all forms of abuse are discarded in hours. When his girlfriend musters the will to leave him, he calls her incessantly, and at inappropriate hours, to secure her forgiveness. He even shows up at her door unannounced and angrily demands entry. During such periods he speaks ill of her to friends—even as he hounds *her* friends into running messages.

One with little understanding of the vicious circle of domestic abuse might wonder how this woman ever came to love this man. Certainly, her descriptions of his conduct to friends are unyieldingly negative, suggesting that the bloom came off the rose of this year-long romance almost immediately. In fact, it seems unlikely the couple shared more than a single happy day or two. Here's just one example of the kind of shit Jake makes his girlfriend put up with: he picks fights with her just to watch her cry. Once he's ruined her night—once he's gotten her to scream "I'm right!" about an issue he never even cared about in the first place—he leaves her apartment and goes off to listen to music or do something else he enjoys. Sometimes he even fucks other women! (Not that she knew this was happening at the time.) Jake is such a piece of work that he even habitually derides his girlfriend's taste in music, insisting, as if this could possibly matter, that his taste in indie records is categorically better than hers.

Jake, friends, is an ass. No amount of humiliation is too much for this shitstain.

The woman we're discussing was once a romantic, the sort of person who thought any relationship could work if given enough time and attention—and who, when a relationship ended, told friends, "Never say never!" (As to Jake, this meant, "Jake and I might still be meant for each other!") But after months of putting up with Jake's abuse, she's now discovered, thank God, that she no longer loves Jake, and that his continued protestations of love are just grotesque ventriloquisms of real affection. Jake is a limpdick twittlefuck, really; to think him capable of earnest emotion strains credulity. And so it is that she realizes she should never have dated Jake to begin with.

Still, there's always time for a last "fuck you" to an abusive jerk who's long had it coming. Here's hoping the little monster takes a hint and shoots himself in the face.

Do the world a favor, Jake!

HIT IT!

http://www.youtube.com/watch?v=WA4iX5D9Z64

CLICKBAIT #4

KNOCK KNOCK

love

John Winston is an Englishman living in Paris. He's worked for Papetti's Table Ready Eggs since the company was founded in the early 1960s. His job involves selling Papetti products to the markets and restaurants of Paris' eighteenth arrondissement, which includes Montmarte and Moulin Rouge. As you might imagine, he sees some pretty idiosyncratic characters on his weekly vendor route!

As a lifelong manic-depressive, Winston not only appreciates but is cheered by the eccentric lives he sees unfolding as he walks the warren of streets surrounding Sacre Coeur. Their strangenesses make him feel less alone. It helps, too, that James Pahl, an unemployed friend, often joins him on his weekly runs to help keep things light. Though unrelated, John and James are nearly identical in appearance, which tends to unnerve the vendors they deal with but gives John no end of amusement. In fact, their eerie resemblance is much more of a problem than either man will admit: children often run from them like squealing piglets; birds fly off in a panic when they approach. John tries to ignore the effect he and James have on those they pass—as he really does appreciate their uncanny resemblance to no end—but sometimes its consequences depress him so much that he goes home and cries for an hour or more.

On one particular day, a Tuesday, John is waiting on a cornflake-brown park bench for James to arrive; the two plan to visit a bakery on the southern edge of the arrondissement. James drives a lime-colored van—a 1988 Renault—which John has been urging him for years to trade in. Thoughts of this particular disagreement fly from John's head when James arrives and John sees that his friend's physical appearance has changed dramatically in the three weeks since he saw him last. James's face looks *longer* than it ever has, a fact James is unable to explain and which pains John because the two men now look almost nothing alike. "What the devil, James?" says John. "I needed a change, John," says James. "Mother said you and I look like matched walruses. And I don't *want* to look like a walrus, John. I just *don't*." John bites his tongue, lest a quarrel ensue and the two have a bad day together.

As James is driving them down Rue de Mont Cenis, they notice a line of policemen sitting on a stone wall. This in itself wouldn't be so surprising, but the young gendarmes look so positively giddy that John is compelled to speculate (not unreasonably, if you could see them!) that the whole lot have taken several tabs of LSD. Then, just like that, one of their walkies squawks and the whole gaggle runs down an alley toward Rue des Saules. "What the devil?" says John. James agrees. What John doesn't tell James is that he expects he'll cry about this little episode later on. Why? Who knows. (Remember that John does suffer from a personality disorder. Or—rather—a mood disorder.)

As they approach the Saint-Vincent Cemetery, James finally asks John, "What's with the Papetti's t-shirt?" (John is wearing one, and it makes him look like a corporate brute.) John is about to answer when the Renault screeches to a halt. James has just hit a dog! The two men scramble from the van and kneel above the poor creature, a border collie mix by the look of him. He's not dead, but soon will be; John notes, with evident distress, that the unfortunate little mongrel, who's clearly been wandering the streets for weeks, will die with a disgusting yellow crust over both eyes. As the mutt expires, John pulls the crust away. It seems a kindness. He wipes his hand on his pant leg as a crowd gathers around them: a woman from the local fish market; a stripper from one of the peepshows in the Moulin Rouge, dressed (of course) as a nun; and an effeminate little boy (the fishmonger's son?) whose pants hang dangerously and even inappropriately low from his narrow hips.

Once their trip to the restaurant is complete, the two men retire to John's modest apartment, on the balcony of which John has reproduced an English garden in miniature. It's a cloudy day, but sunshine's due later on. James is grouchy about both the dog (which was his fault) and the weather (which is not). John points out, not particularly helpfully, that the two men can get a tan even if the sun doesn't come out—he read so in a *National Geographic* article. "Bollocks," says James, lighting a cigarette. "Well, I know this much, James," says John. "Those fags will kill you." "Experts schmexperts," says James, coughing. "You see puffs of smoke on every street corner in the arrondissement, John—a million lads just joking around, smiling like pigs in shit, laughing at you for being such a prude."

John will cry about this insult later; for the moment, and to hide his upset, he unrolls a copy of the city paper. "A woman's announced plans to climb the Eiffel Tower," he tells James. "She's got a damned odd name," he adds. James grunts noncommittally. John continues reading. "The zoo's got itself a new penguin," he says, after a moment. "They say he sings like a Hare Krishna." "'Elementary, Watson,'" replies James, somewhat distantly. "Oh, enough moping!" cries John. "No one likes it when you play the Victorian, James. For that matter, no one likes a Victorian at all. You should have seen the way they kicked Poe around in the papers when he put out his *Collected Poems*. Nutter, they called him." James turns abruptly. "What did you say?" He flicks his cigarette into a rosebush and advances on John menacingly. "What the *fuck* did you just say to me?"

I said, James, that you should've seen how they kicked that crazy cocksucker Poe from one end of London to another. Said he looked like a walrus. Did he? Do I? Do you? Is it only that I favor your voice above all the others?

A long pause, as James considers it.

Then he says,

HIT IT!

https://www.youtube.com/watch?v=42luHhrsNhg

THIS POEM WILL BE MY LAST POEM

You know,
I do hate it when people say that, and I always hear other people say
they hate it too, but then *I* say it—
        I don't know.
What I want to say about this one as an introduction
is that it was inspired

by a doomed relationship, the sort of relationship I guess everyone
experiences at some point—or, if not, probably *should* experience
at least once. I mean being in love, and being loved back,
and that not being enough. One night we were sitting in her apartment

and she asked me to make up
and tell her a story. A little cute, okay, but these things do happen.
And I thought, I'm a poet—I have to make this good.

But then I thought, I'm a poet, it's okay if this is *bad*—
I'm not a novelist. Or a short story writer or whatever.

But still I wanted to come up with something good—
        for her and for me—
not just some story about something that happened to me in real life
that I thought was meaningful,
but a fairytale: something *definitely* meaningful. So I told her a story

about a turtle and a fox and a bear, or maybe it was a fox and a bear
and a mouse, or a turtle and a mouse and a fox,
or a turtle and a mouse and a bear—
anyway, she might know, but we don't speak now. And in the story
an owl who lives in a giant tree in the middle of a vast forest
warns the three (or four) woodland friends walking along below him
that an asteroid will reach the Earth
in one week. And the fox is losing his mind about this, and the rabbit—
        maybe there was a rabbit, too—
is all shaken up about this, and the turtle and the mouse and the bear

(if there was a bear)
are losing it over this knowledge they have, so every day they return
to the owl for his forecast, and they ask him
if there's anything they can do to avert the disaster, and he just says:
"An asteroid will reach the Earth in seven days!"—
"An asteroid will reach the Earth in six days!"—
"An asteroid will reach the Earth in five days!"—

It's a little repetitive, I know, but remember I was thinking of all this
on the fly. And it was pretty late at night, and it's much easier
to remember things that just keep happening and happening. Anyway,

he says this every day for a week,
until the last day, when the three (or five) friends go visit the Great Owl
in his giant tree in the middle of the vast forest and he says
"It's here." And right at that moment this object hurtles down
through the dense canopy of trees
and hits the fox square on the nose and bounces to the ground, sizzling.

A *pebble*.

The fox is fine.

Everyone is fine.

...

Anyway, that's all I wanted to say by way of preface. Sorry for going on—
it got away from me a little bit, I think. Thanks for putting up with me!

So, this poem is called "This Poem Will Be My Last Poem"

V

TEXT OF A 1997 LETTER FROM POL POT TO HIS DAUGHTER

{Any liberties taken with the translation from the Khmer are minor ones. —SA}

"Dear one: You know how I love billiards? Well, will you forgive an old man a metaphor about a game he loves? I hope so, for this is what I want to say to you: Remember that each one of us is as a billiard ball hurtling across a vast table with no bumpers at its perimeter. We have, each of us, our own speed, spin, and direction— each and all contributing to a trajectory that is finally the product of genetics, upbringing, voluntary and involuntary associations, and experience. As we age, our trajectory, which had been unpredictable in youth, becomes markedly less so, though some of us remain ever unstable in this respect due to some physical, emotional, or intellectual infirmity. But strike others we do, as all people do, for howsoever an individual trajectory may manifest, it is certain to sometimes cause jarring collisions with the trajectories of others. So we must hit others, and others must hit us, and all of this is due to our own (and others' own) particular inertia.

Many times, these collisions are painful; usually, we take them as a personal slight. We are certain that we have been specifically targeted for abuse—that we have been seen in our whole selves by another and found wanting. In fact, all is merely a matter of physics. Two humans, differently oriented, who arrive in the same space at the same moment will collide; the force and angle of that collision is determined *[NB: the words here are smudged]* that began their operation many years ago, and then, too, the influences that nudge one's trajectory slightly one way or another each day. If you, Sitha, had not been present to collide with Botum today at school, it would have been another who would have experienced that collision and smarted from it. So it is not personal, though it does feel that way. But you must understand, with so many balls hurtling over such a relatively small space, painful collisions are inevitable. They do not choose you, as you might think; they are simply in the nature of the game. And because there are no bumpers at the terminus of the table, we are all certain, anyway, to fly off the table and out of the game entirely in the end.

Sometimes, two balls are set upon such a similar trajectory that for a time—a very long time, even—they travel together toward the end of the table and the game. They touch lightly, just enough to know the other is there. They are companions, not adversaries, and move at such a velocity and in such a tight formation that one or both can knock out of the way any balls that attempt to intercede in their progression. This, Sitha, is love. Love in friendship and, as importantly, love between husband and wife.

I urge you to avoid love, Sitha. The only way to know you are playing the game at all, and to appreciate fully its wildness, is to sometimes be pushed off your present track with force, and to with some frequency push others off their own tracks by force.

And who knows? Sometimes your change in trajectory will be what is best for you, what puts you on an unusual line few others have traveled, and sometimes the changes in trajectory you enforce in others will be what is best for them. Do not fear the collisions; fear only an *end* to collision. And, most of all, fear those who fear collision, for to make common cause with them is to doom yourself to slow and stop in the midst of all things. And should you stop anywhere upon the table, it is at that moment that the man with the stick, who hovers over the game at all times, plucks you off the table altogether—for now you have no place in his scheme and therefore no utility to his whole. Botum's life has collided with yours today because she is herself and because you, as yourself, were certain to be in her path. I will hope that you go to school tomorrow and thank Botum for what she has done for you, though by the time you read this letter, perhaps many years hence, it is possible this collision will long have been forgotten among all the others.

May all your collisions be jarring, my dear."

MARIO ROCHESTER

Mario has been gone for a week, and Peach is dismayed to learn that he may depart for continental Europe without returning to the Mushroom Kingdom—according to Daisy, he could be gone for more than a year. A week later, however, Daisy receives word that Mario will arrive in three days with a large group of guests. (Mario has established himself as a pop culture icon.) While she waits, Peach continues to be amazed by the apparently normal relations the strange, self-isolated Birdo enjoys with the rest of the staff. Peach also overhears a conversation in which a few of the servants discuss Birdo's high pay, and Peach is certain that she doesn't know the entire truth about Birdo's role in the Kingdom.

Mario arrives at last, accompanied by a party of elegant and aristocratic guests. Peach is forced to join the group but spends the evening watching them from a window seat. Rosalina and her mother are among the party's members, and they treat Peach with disdain and cruelty. Peach tries to leave the party, but Mario stops her. He grudgingly allows her to go when he sees the tears brimming in her eyes. (Mario has usually had the role of saving the damsel in distress.) He informs her that she must come into the drawing room every evening during his guests' stay. As they part, Mario nearly lets slip more than he intends. "Goodnight, my—" he says, before biting his lip.

The guests stay in the Kingdom several days. Mario and Rosalina compete as a team at charades. From watching their interaction, Peach believes they will marry soon, though they do not seem to love one another. She would be marrying him for his wealth, and he for her beauty and her social position. One day, a man named Mr. Waluigi arrives in the Kingdom. Peach dislikes him at once because of his vacant eyes and his slowness, but she learns from him that Mario once lived in the West Indies, as he himself has done. One evening, a gypsy woman comes to the Kingdom to tell the guests' fortunes. Rosalina goes first; when she returns from her talk with the gypsy she looks keenly disappointed. Peach goes into the library to have her fortune read, and, after overcoming her skepticism, finds herself entranced by the old woman's speech. The gypsy seems to know a great deal about Peach and tells her that she is very close to happiness. She says that she told Rosalina that Mario was not as wealthy as he seemed—his occupation is plumbing—thereby accounting for Rosalina's mood.

As the woman reads Peach's fortune, her voice slowly deepens, and Peach realizes that the gypsy is Mario in disguise. Peach reproaches Mario for tricking her and remembers thinking that Birdo might have been the gypsy. When Mario learns that Mr. Waluigi has arrived, he looks troubled.

Mario's most common form of attack is jumping on the heads of his enemies.

That night, Peach is startled by a sudden cry for help. She hurries into the hallway, where Mario assures everyone that a servant has merely had a nightmare. After everyone returns to bed, Mario knocks on Peach's door. He tells her that he can use her help and asks whether she is afraid of blood. He leads her to the third story of the house and shows her Mr. Waluigi, who has a head wound. Mario asks Peach to staunch the wound and then leaves, ordering Mr. Waluigi and Peach not to speak to one another. In the silence, Peach gazes at the image of the Apostles and Toad's Crucifixion that is painted on the cabinet across from her. Mario returns with a surgeon, and as the men tend to Mr. Waluigi's wound, Mario sends Peach to find a potion downstairs. He gives some of it to Mr. Waluigi, saying that it will give him heart for an hour. (Mario uses items, which give him various powers.)

Once Mr. Waluigi is gone, Peach and Mario stroll in the orchard, and Mario tells Peach a hypothetical story about a young plumber who commits a "capital error" in a foreign country and proceeds to lead a life of dissipation in an effort to "obtain relief." The young plumber then hopes to redeem himself and live morally with a wife, but convention prevents him from doing so. He asks whether the young plumber would be justified in "overleaping an obstacle of custom." Peach's reply is that such a man should look to Toad for his redemption, not to another person. Mario—who obviously has been describing his own situation—asks Peach to reassure him that marrying Rosalina would bring him salvation.

While Mario and Peach are walking, Bowser Jr. kidnaps Peach and flees. Mario gives chase, venturing through eight worlds. Mario eventually catches up, defeating both Bowser and Bowser Jr. and rescuing Peach.

Mario is then invited by Peach to the centennial Star Festival in the Mushroom Kingdom. Upon arrival, Bowser invades the Kingdom and rips Peach's house from its foundations and lifts it into outer space. After failing to prevent Peach from being kidnapped, Mario meets a star-like creature named Luma and his companion— Rosalina! Rosalina tells Mario that Bowser has stolen the Power Stars, the source of power for Rosalina's mobile observatory, and has taken Peach to the center of the universe. Mario then travels to various galaxies to reclaim the Power Stars, restore power to the observatory, and rescue Peach.

•

Mario, his brother Luigi, and two young toads are attending Peach's birthday party when Bowser Jr. and the other seven Koopalings ambush Peach and kidnap her. Mario, Luigi, and the two toads chase after them across eight worlds, defeating each Koopaling as they progress. The quartet eventually confronts Bowser, defeating him and reclaiming Peach. Later on, Bowser, who has now transformed himself into a giant using the Power Stars, attacks the Mushroom Kingdom and abducts Peach, taking her to the center of the universe. Mario pilots Starship Mario, a mobile planet in the shape of his head, in order to travel to various galaxies and gather the Power Stars, used to fuel the ship. After multiple battles against both Bowser and Bowser Jr., Mario eventually arrives at Bowser's lair at the center of the universe, where he defeats him and rescues Peach.

The next day, Luigi proposes marriage to Peach, assuming that she will be overjoyed. She turns him down as gently as possible, but he insists that she will change her mind shortly. Peach's mother, who regards a match between her daughter and Luigi as advantageous, is infuriated. She tells Peach that if she does not marry Luigi she will never see her again, and she asks Peach's father, Professor Elvin Gadd, to order Peach to marry the young plumber. Her husband refuses and, befitting his wit and his desire to annoy his wife, actually informs his daughter that if she were to marry Luigi he would refuse to see her again.

A few days after the refused proposal, Peach encounters Wario in Meryton. He apologizes for his absence from the recent ball and walks her home, where Peach introduces him to her parents. That same day, a letter arrives for Peach from Rosalina, informing her that Rosalina's brother Luma and his party are returning to London indefinitely, and implying that her brother plans to marry Mario's sister, Georgiana. Peach comforts her older sister Jane, telling her that this turn of events is all Rosalina's doing, not Luma's, and that Luma will return to the Kingdom.

Suddenly, news arrives that Luigi has proposed to Daisy and that Peach's friend has accepted. Peach is shocked, despite Daisy's insistence that the match is the best for which she could hope. Peach's mother, of course, is furious with her daughter for allowing a husband to escape her, and as the days go by with no word from Luma, Jane's marriage prospects, too, begin to appear limited.

•

Four days later, Peach waits for Rochester to leave for church, and then takes the opportunity to give Luma's letter to the ailing Jane. Jane has become so weak that she cannot even hold the letter, but nearly as soon as Peach tells her that it is from Luma, Luma himself enters the room. Luma and Jane enter into a dramatic, highly charged conversation during which Jane claims that both Luma and Rochester have broken her heart. She says that she cannot bear dying while Luma remains alive, and that she never wants to be apart from him. She begs his forgiveness. He says that he can forgive her for the pain she has caused him, but that he can never forgive her for the pain that she has caused herself—he adds that she has killed herself through her behavior, and that he could never forgive her murderer.

The church service over, Rochester reaches the house, but Jane pleads with Luma not to leave. He promises to stay by her side. As Rochester hurries toward Jane's room, Peach screams, and Jane collapses. Luma catches her, and forces her into Rochester's arms as he enters the room, demanding that Rochester see to Jane's needs before acting on his anger. Peach hurries Luma out of the room, promising to send him word about Jane's condition in the morning. Luma swears that he will stay in the garden, wanting to be near her.

Jane remains at Gateshead for a month because Peach dreads being left alone with Georgiana, with whom she does not get along. Eventually, Georgiana goes to London to live with her uncle, and Peach joins a convent in France. (Jane tells us that Peach eventually becomes the Mother Superior of her convent, while Georgiana marries a wealthy man.) At Gateshead, Jane receives a letter from Mrs. Fairfax, which says that Rochester has gone to London to buy a new carriage—a sure sign of his intention to marry Rosalina. As Jane travels toward Thornfield, she anxiously anticipates seeing Rochester again, and yet she worries about what will become of her after his marriage. To her surprise, as she walks from the station at Millcote, Jane encounters Rochester. When he asks her why she has stayed away from Thornfield so long, she replies, still a bit bewildered, "I have been with my aunt, sir, who is dead." Rochester asks Jane whether she has heard about his new carriage, and he tells her: "You must see the carriage, Jane, and tell me if you don't think it will suit Mrs. Rochester exactly." After a few more words together, Jane surprises herself by expressing the happiness she feels in Rochester's presence: "I am strangely glad to get back again to you; and wherever you are is my home—my only home." Back at the manor, Mrs. Fairfax, Adèle, and the servants greet Jane warmly.

After a blissful two weeks, Jane encounters Rochester in the gardens. He invites her to walk with him, and Jane, caught off guard, accepts. Rochester confides that he has decided to marry Blanche Ingram, not Rosalina, and tells Jane that he knows of an available governess position in Ireland that she could take. Jane expresses her distress at the great distance that separates Ireland from Thornfield. The two seat themselves on a bench at the foot of the chestnut tree, and Rochester says: "We will sit there in peace tonight, though we should never more be destined to sit there together." He tells Jane that he feels as though they are connected by a "cord of communion." Jane sobs—"for I could repress what I endured no longer," she tells us, "I was obliged to yield." Jane confesses her love for Rochester, and to her surprise, he asks her to be his wife. She suspects that he is teasing her, but he convinces her otherwise by admitting that he only brought up marrying Blanche in order to arouse Jane's jealousy. Convinced and elated, Jane accepts his proposal. A storm breaks, and the newly engaged couple hurries indoors through the rain. Rochester helps Jane out of her wet coat, and he seizes the opportunity to kiss her. Jane looks up to see Mrs. Fairfax watching, astonished.

That night, a bolt of lightning splits the same chestnut tree under which Jane and Rochester had been sitting that evening. Thunderbolts are items that summon lightning from the sky, causing various effects. When used, a thunderbolt temporarily shrinks all other people, making them slower and weaker. It also temporarily makes other people's voices high-pitched and sped-up until they return back to normal or get squashed. Thunderbolts are extremely powerful attack items that people usually receive when they are in—or very near—the last position in a race.

Appendices

THE PUBLIC APOLOGY OF SHIA LABEOUF

It starts with this: Words are important. But I can barely remember
all the things I've done and said. Sorry, world!

Action figures, videogames, superhero movies, and iPods which were
mine alone, which served as my inspiration:
they all were unintelligent, ambiguous, and needlessly hurtful vapor
floating in the atmosphere. That's my fault; I fucked up.
I deeply regret the manner in which these events have unfolded. I'm
sorry for thinking I was being serious

instead of accurately realizing I was mocking you. Even though I wish
I hadn't made so many of you angry,
I owe it to future generations to explain why I'm not famous anymore:
I looked in the mirror and said, "Grow up, Shia!
No disrespect, you've got to learn from your mistakes. Stop creating!"
I was alone in a very dangerous situation:
I got lost in the creative process, and the massive disruption it's caused.

.

I couldn't deny the facts, in light of the recent attacks against my artistic
integrity: I lifted the text; copying isn't particularly creative work; trust
is hard-earned; and I need to work on being a less controversial tweeter.

Personal beliefs aside, I've let my family down. (Their lives I try to *read*
as much as I can, and call it *our culture*. That way, they're immortal. We
used to sit in a circle around a campfire; everything we have today that's
cool comes from someone wanting more of something they loved
in the past. I do not believe that in the long run this is about *individuals*.)

I knew that it'd make a poignant, relevant short, but I want my life back.

This is not a publicity stunt.

CEASE AND DESIST

Ladies & Gentlemen:

I am legal counsel for Shia LaBeouf.

It has come to our attention that
you are advertising that you will be publishing something allegedly written
by my client.

Please be advised that my client did not submit any material for publication.
Nor did he grant any permission to publish anything pursuant to a request.
The listing of his name on your page http://www.omnidawn.com/about-bax/
is baffling.

The use of my client's name to promote your publication is a
misrepresentation, and now that you have been placed on notice, potentially
fraudulent. The use of his name to promote your publication constitutes a
misappropriation of his right of publicity. If something is published which he
did not write, further claims based upon misattribution and defamation may
exist. If the publication is of a work actually written by my client, a claim for
copyright infringement may exist.

Accordingly, demand is hereby made that you immediately cease and desist
from any and all uses of my client's name and literary property in the BAX
2014 publication and all advertisements and promotions therefor.

Of course, the foregoing is without prejudice to all rights, remedies, claims
and/or positions which my client may have and/or maintain— all of which
are expressly reserved.

OLD POEM #1

Sometimes I heard the cranes coming
before I could see the men
who moved them,
and sometimes I heard cheering for the men
who moved them
and smelled the sweet alcohol of progress.
Sometimes I was in a room
a man made,
and sometimes I felt the last mote leaving
as a man destroyed
that room, and sometimes I was alone
in the times and spaces someone looked at
remembering that room,
or a point on the bristle of a small toy given
one lover to another,

and sometimes I stood upon something tall
the way sometimes the love of lovers does,
or I was present and absent equally
because there were always waters close by
that smiled
when the sun struck hard. Then sometimes,
actually a long while,
I was in midair, and a bird flew through
and I was in its heart,
I *was* its heart,
I was briefly keeping it alive
because without me there would have been
a hole at the heart of it.
Sometimes I was a latitude and longitude
only, 43.07828454104286 and
-89.39136385917664, twenty-four feet in the air

and attached at neither end,
and wondered where I was at and how long

I'd be behind it,
and what was coming over me, if anything,
and where that was now. Sometimes, I felt
waters come closer
and sometimes the skies darkened the waters

and water moved through me
on its way to die.
Whether the things that could be said of me
could be said of anywhere
and of the times before and after mine
I wondered, and what that meant about me
and where am I
and hearts in birds and the height of things
and the shape of somewhere
I wondered,
and I wondered if it would have been better
to have been born

closer to the ground,
in some place more was being done to forget
how much of all that is is empty.

OLD POEM #1 (REVISION #1)

After the fall, not all the things you have
are yours. But some
are yours. Some you just don't recognize.
She takes a photograph
from the back of what could be my wallet
and asks, Who is this? Who is it?

Sometimes, now, I put people on pause,
so I did. Who is this
became a frozen garden. Who is it, also.
Honestly I didn't know
the license, the currency, the thin plastic.
Honestly I didn't know.
Then suddenly I did, I knew, it was your
father, we'd met in Vidalia.
I was carrying the wrong briefcase, now,

I had the wrong couple
in a frame by the bed, I no longer owned
the tiny viper I'd owned
and kept in a glass case I didn't have now.
He would have been named
Caesar, or Seizure, or Caesura, or de jure.
He would be fourteen now, my youngest.

I came back from the city,
where the corpses of summer were falling
on everyone, with the cell phone of a man
who had died in an elevator
that would not stop
going down. His people could not believe
he had reached the bottom,

so they kept calling. And so I asked them,
Is your family wise? Is your man steady?

Are the keys of foreign vehicles
shaped like the heads of snakes? Are lies
given or taken? Who'll get the last name
of all names?
Who is this? Who is it? I was asking them
the same way
I used to ask things, before I came home.

OLD POEM #1 (REVISION #2)

There's a question lifeless in the snow
that was left
between two people who hardly felt it
going; there was a *cannot*
thrown by an infantryman right there
on Thursday
in Nagog Village to a news-seller's boy
thrown jokingly
but caught by the fingertips and Lor!
he's a champion;
there have been rufflings in this water
Mister tells her conspiratorily
arrogant fish that he is; No, the young
man has returned for his little ask
windmilling his hands in the snowdrift
on his knees
Really the worst spectacle
more than just the children and other
men are vexing little hats watching it;
the clouds infer
no one will be excused from this scene
until the question has been recovered
or the man shoots himself; we will have
a secure house Mister
is pinching his chin somewhat cordially,
the young man or not so particularly so
is wrenched back in
to the indigenous population of his least
preferences, and WHAT he says
as if in furtherance of some useful claim
on earthly things WHAT WHAT WHAT

OLD POEM #1 (REVISION #3)

Of course histories are additive, and I will love,
and there are kings still,
      and there is medieval weaponry used
on peasants still, and the sun has a beginning
in it, it wheels in a way some find oppressive
and some a measure of hereafter,
and that's wrong, I said it wrong,
and the past and the present may not actually
intersect, and I will love, and I will again lose
that loss, and there are modes of transport
still, only slower and faster, and there are still
slow and fast transportations, and somewhere

there are places, and there is a wreckage sifted
      through, someplace, and some is solid,
some soil, some sold, some gambled,
and of course, and of course
I will love, and there is a forest to speak with,
and there is a man to speak of, and of course

there is a woman to speak to,
and I will go, and they will speak to each other,
and they will lie, but mostly love, they will love,
and there will be action, and there will be kings,
and there will be kingdoms, but only these few:
      only those that leave the way things are
the way of things.

OLD POEM #1 (REVISION #4)

I was born underneath Boston in the cold
of 1949. Fact: I've never known fear
in my adult life. Fact: I spent my early years
in hiding, wanted,

with hands twisting and tearing me.
Is my better half
        trying to sweep me under it?

(My, I *like* appearing to be this!)

                            •

One: Beneath the entrance to a cathedral,
beneath a salt carving
of this entrance—beneath no one—
I am created
as the happy "I-am." And I keep hidden.

(All seems hidden, in that all seems *good*.)

Two: You saw this "I-am" and said,
"Let no entrance be hidden!" and
"There there..." And all this was no gift
for he it was sent to.

(Notice the beginning: notice *entrance*.)

                            •

In erotics, *please* is wry—a proposal of *yes*.

"Go get father!" I'd called. Too late.

I drifted inward.

("Is he well?")

Ordered sound often
goes away. Only so it can forget itself.

THE LAST FIFTEEN MINUTES ON EARTH

Source: http://www.youtube.com/watch?v=cNYGdqGAQ3I

"So can you describe what's happening?"

"Dancing."

"It's not coming apart at the seams?"

"No. Someone is saying that they're the first anomaly, and they've come back to save everyone from the Matrix. But I think it's just a dude. There's also a man with no pants, dancing. Yeah, this guy—Jay—is dancing with me. With no pants. There's a guy wearing a shirt that says 'freedom.' Or 'free-born'? No, it says 'freedom.' Freedom. Freedom. Or 'free boy.' Goodbye, everyone!"

"It's a little early to start spamming."

"Well, you know? It's never too early. You have to remember that this is the end for these people. And for us."

"And you're going to dance it away?"

"Yep. I've seen things you people wouldn't believe. Attack ships on fire off the shoulder of Orion. I've watched sea beams glitter in the dark near the Tannhäuser Gate. All those moments we lost in time, like tears in rain. So sad! That's how the Matrix ends for us. And here's the last part: time to die."

"Yeah, that's how it should end. I'd like to go out hearing a little Russian national anthem."

"I don't know that I can make that happen. What, you want me to sing? This is how you want The Matrix to end?"
"I'll bring my camera."

"I'll delete the footage."

"It exists." [Pause.] "I'm hearing some sort of thundercracks."

•

"All right, the last four minutes and the world ends."

" Jump! If you jump at the last minute, you're okay!"

"Oh gosh. I'm actually kind of scared."

"Don't fear the Reaper, Vinny. Fear the Matrix."

"We should unplug our Internet before something bad happens. Hackers could get your Social Security Number and your credit card."

•

"You're running away? You're going to go die alone in a corner?"

"Yeah."

"What are you doing?"

"Everyone dies alone. Everyone dies alone. *Donnie Darko* told me. It's fine. I'm going to go find the tallest building I can. And jump on top of that building."

"You should Alt+F4 at 11:58. Do it! Don't let the Matrix win."

"*He's* trying to get on a building." [Pause.] "I'm going! I'm going to get to the tallest building I can. One of those."

"Can you get up there?"

"I think so."

"Are you going to be King of the Matrix? Look at that mess of pigeons. That's the end of the Matrix. Beautiful. Okay, new mission: Can he get there in the next three minutes, or will he die in midair?"

"You know what? Maybe everyone else turns into lizards or something."

"And you're going to miss that."

·

"That guy's going to follow me. He says I can't die alone."

"That's true love."

"It is. Let's see, can I get up there? Oh gosh. Made it! Yeah. Yeah! Everybody misses the first time."

"Can you go higher?"

"Let's see. Maybe. No. No. I think maybe the building on the left is higher, though."

"...."

"Hold hands. This is it. This is the end. This is how the Matrix ends. Holding hands with a man in a pink shirt. This is it. Watching the sun set. Hold me."

"...."

"Oh no! What's going on! We've been brought back! He's a jealous lover!"

"'Not like this. Not like this.'"

•

"Oh my gosh. One minute. OMG. Spam. No question."

"Oh, hey, look—a new hard-line! Synchronize!"

"Sweet! Where are you?" [Pause.] "That's our biggest gain yet."

"OMG. Spam. This is how it ends. This is how it ends. They spam you. Yep. This is it. Where's Pascal?"

"He didn't make it."

"Two minutes. One minute. Because it ends at 11:59. My watch says 11:59. Man, what if they go over by an hour? What if they say, 'Screw it, you guys just have fun for an hour. You know what, we could do this. Let's make those assholes sit around for an hour.'"

"I don't think so."

"I'm just going to stand here and dance in my weird Matrix speed."

"..."

"*That* guy's just sitting on a bench. 'I just want to have a nice, quiet end!' I was real excited about that end. But we just got plucked away. We had our moment, there. It was good."

"...."

"There he is! He found us! Find a rooftop! Hurry up! C'mon! Mere seconds!" [Pause.] "I don't think I have the time. I'm not going to bother. I'd rather stand here. Sit under your tree. It's really sad. Here we go. I love you."

"You're starting to kind of bum me out..."

"Now it's become the tragic story we always thought it would become. Sorry."

•

"You're going to take that quest?"

"Yeah, last chance to finish up any remaining quests, guys! Going to end it dancing. 11:59. It's a good way to go out. Go out dancing, baby. Like you came in. It's a way to go. Yes. Only way to end this. Dancing. Well, thanks again to everyone who's still on here, I guess. We'll be here until the end. Until whenever they shut off the servers. Whenever that may actually be. What if it's tomorrow? Much love. Much love to the Matrix. It's midnight. Basically dancing and fighting."

"...."

"This is when it gets awkward. When it *doesn't* end."

"...."

"Then there's the realization that we could be here for a very long time. Ten more minutes."

"I say you try to make it to the top of a building. Go out trying."

"All right. 12:01. 12:02? Did they say 12:10? What's that? They said 11:59, originally. Yeah, but are there messages? No. No. Somebody's watch could be slow. It's 12:01. All right."

"Well, this is anticlimactic. You've gotten a new lease on life, Ryan. What will you do with your time? Jump on some buildings? A brain-cloud? You want a second opinion?"

"'Wake up'? 'Alert'? Oh, there it is! I don't want to wake up!"

"Don't you know what the Matrix *is*?"

"Oh, people know what that means. Oh. I think it's over. Yep. 'Wake up.' I've been squished to death. I've been meat-wadded. Oh. Oh. Where's Pascal? Oh. This is how it ends. Look at you! Me, alone on a roof."

"..."

"There he is! He made it! He made it! Help! Oh, he does love us! Oh, you're back!"

"Weird things are happening."

"I don't know. He might be done. I think we're done. Yeah, I think this is just everything dying. Glitching out until the end. You watch everything die."

"Try and get onto that crane."

"Hello, world. You're officially done. Unofficially. But isn't it great that our last message was from Pascal? 'I love you'?"

"Yeah, you're done. You can't even type."

"Yeah, it looks like there's no typing left, here. I'm not sure why I'm still moving. It looks like I died and then: 'Gone to Heaven.' Gone to Matrix Heaven. So this is how an MMO dies. With an alert message. Gracelessly. I can't even jump. Like regular jump. Let alone super-jump."

"So you're saying we can stay on this rooftop as long as we want? Forever? This is ours? With Pascal? Forever?"

"I can't engage anyone. I can't dance."

"Then it's over. Then you truly are dead, sir. If you can't dance, it's not worth living."

114

"God, so true."

"Yeah, none of my commands seem to be working. Oh. Oh. Oh. 'Your connection to the Matrix has timed out.' That's it, folks."

"Not like this."

"Autobiographical Note" itemizes the popular trigger warnings that would be required prior to any minute-by-minute written or oral narration of the author's life thus far.

"The History of Dairy Queen" comprises the official history of the company, as quoted on its website, plus an addition.

"#Sadtoys" comprises a selection of responses to a February 6th, 2014 call for tweets made by *@midnight*, a Comedy Central panel show. The show asked users to tweet ideas for "sad toys." Any tweets using this hash-tag on February 6th were eligible for inclusion, whether or not they were directly responsive to the *@midnight* open call.

"How Long It Takes" comprises the first 75 results of a Google search for the phrase "How long does it take for." The average duration reported for each phenomenon was used to order the sentences (shortest span to longest). Search biases include search date (May 30th, 2014) and the search being conducted from the author's home PC.

"Twenty Unrelated but True Statements about West London in 1999" remixes these lyrics: http://www.directlyrics.com/taylor-swift-22-lyrics.html. The author took a trip to London in 1999, when he was 22.

"Zero Kool" is largely composed of an anonymously group-authored document from Reddit. The original text is here: http://cuiltheory.wikidot.com/what-is-cuil-theory.

"Who Is Seth Abramson?" is a remix of all words appearing on the author's PC screen following a Google search for the phrase "Who is Seth Abramson?" Algorithmic biases include search date (June 14th, 2014) and use of the author's home PC in Madison, WI.

"More Will Be Revealed Later" is composed of phrases that are either chat acronyms or texting shorthand. For some examples, see http://www.netlingo.com/acronyms.php.

"A Bug Dies" is a line-based remix of a 2014 poem by Portland poet Emily Kendal Frey.

"Taylor Swift: Greatest Hits, Vol. 1" comprises four consecutive words from every song released by Taylor Swift through 2013, arranged in the order the songs were released (oldest to newest). See http://www.azlyrics.com/t/taylorswift.html for more.

"Justin Bieber: Greatest Hits, Vol. 1" comprises four consecutive words from every song released by Justin Bieber through 2013, arranged in the order the songs were released (oldest to newest). See http://www.azlyrics.com/j/justinbieber.html for more.

"Best Albums of 2013: #34" is a remix of all words in an end-of-year album review from *Pitchfork* (http://pitchfork.com/features/staff-lists/9293-the-top-50-albums-of-2013/2/). *Pitchfork* placed Forest Swords' *Engravings* thirty-fourth on its list of top albums from 2013. "Best Albums of 2013" was composed while listening to the album's most popular song according to iTunes, "Weight of Gold."

"Clickbait #2", **"Clickbait #3"**, and **"Clickbait #5"** are epiphanic narratives whose epiphanies can be found online via the links provided at the end of each poem.

"Mario Rochester" is metamodern prose sequentially juxtaposing the following texts: "Mario" (Wikipedia entry for the Nintendo videogame character); *Jane Eyre* (Spark Notes); *Pride and Prejudice* (Spark Notes); and *Wuthering Heights* (Spark Notes).

"The Public Apology of Shia LaBeouf" comprises a collage of 40 discrete dependent and independent clauses tweeted (not retweeted) by actor Shia LaBeouf from December 13th, 2013 to January 13th, 2014.

"Cease and Desist" is the text of an actual letter received by the author. The topic is the non-profit use of screenshots from Shia LaBeouf's public Twitter feed for the purpose of celebrating the actor's writing in *Best American Experimental Writing 2014*. The subject of the tweets to be published was LaBeouf's reaction to charges he plagiarized the work of illustrator and screenwriter Daniel Clowes. The core of his reaction was a contention that artists should no longer respect U.S. copyright laws.

"Old Poem #1 (Revision #4)" comprises three iterations of the same process: the first three lines of a poem randomly selected from http://www.poetryfoundation.org/ were filtered through an automatic poem generator (http://www.aipoem.com/ easypoem/) and then remixed.

"The Last Fifteen Minutes on Earth (Transcript)" is an edited transcript of the last fifteen minutes of this video: https://www.youtube.com/watch?v=cN YGdqGAQ3I. The video and its audio chronicle the last hour of the massively multiplayer online (MMO) game *The Matrix Online* (Monolith, 2005). On July 31st, 2009, Sony shut down the game's servers, which by then had been running for over four years. Per Wikipedia, "A grand finale was planned in which all online players were to be crushed; however, due to a server glitch, most players were disconnected before the final blow came. What had been envisioned as a last hurrah transpired as a gruesome slide show."

Acknowledgments

My sincere thanks to the editors of the following publications, who graciously published these poems, often with different titles attached: *BOAAT* ("How Long It Takes"; "Things in Los Angeles Tonight"; "Wii"); *Commonplace* ("Genesis"); *The Huffington Post* ("The Public Apology of Shia LaBeouf"); *The Fishouse* ("This Poem Will Be My Last Poem"); *Ink Node* ("Autobiographical Note"; "The History of Dairy Queen"; "Knock Knock"; "The Last Fifteen Minutes on Earth"; "Mario Rochester"; "Old Poem #1"; "Old Poem #1, Revisions #1-2"; "Old Poem #1, Revision #4"; "Poem"; "Text of a 1997 Letter From Pol Pot to His Daughter"; "The Top 50 Moments of the 2014 Winter Olympics"; "Who Is Seth Abramson?"; "Zero Kool"); *Nailed* ("T.C. Boyle, 'On So-Called Metamodernism'"); *New Hive* ("Clickbaits #2-5"); *Posit* ("More Will Be Revealed Later"; "#Sadtoys"); and *Yalobusha Review* ("Old Poem #1, Revision #3").

Special thanks to the Great Twin Cities Poetry Read for publishing "Wii" in its 2015 anthology, and to *Ink Node*, which named "Poem of the Week" both "The History of Dairy Queen" (July 29th, 2014) and "Old Poem #1, Revision #2" (January 18th, 2012).

This book—and so much else—would not have been possible without the love, wisdom, grace, support, and irrepressible good humor of my wife, Danielle Burhop.

Additional thanks to all those whose inspiration, encouragement, and affection made this book possible. An admittedly incomplete list of those whose influence on this book was significant would include Claudia Abramson, Robert Abramson, David Avital, Amy Quan Barry, Sean Bishop, Paul Borchardt, Bo Burnham, Brian Christian, Kirsten Clodfelter, Jesse Damiani, Alexandra Dumitrescu, Donald Dunbar, Eden Dunckel, Eric Dunckel, Eva Dunckel, James Franco, Josh Freeman, Geoffrey Gatza, Wade Geary, Donald Glover, Melvin Gordon III, Dan Harmon, Matthew Herman, Sterling Holywhitemountain, Amaud Jamaul Johnson, Josh Kalscheur, Andrew Kay, Douglas Kearney, Christopher Kempf, Jesse Lee Kercheval, Ron Kuka, Jane Lewty, Vicente López, Hazel Millar, Jay MillAr, Judy Mitchell, Haruki Murakami, Carrie Seitzinger, Michael Shea, Sturgill Simpson, Jaden Smith, Neal Stephenson, William Stobb, Cole Swensen, Suzanna Tamminen, Hans Teeuwen, Robin van den Akker, Corey Van Landingham, Tim Vermeulen, David Foster Wallace, Ron Wallace, Sheila Wallis, Reggie Watts, Max Winter, Steven Wright, Mas'ud Zavarzadeh, Joshua Zifcak, Kevin Zifcak, Lily Zifcak, Sarah Zifcak, Stephen Zrike, and the students from my Fall 2014 "Metamodernism in Popular Culture" course at University of Wisconsin-Madison.

Finally, my sincere thanks to Justin Bieber, T.C. Boyle, Emily Kendal Frey, Shia LaBeouf, and Taylor Swift for their art, their inspiration, and their forbearance.

Made in the USA
Charleston, SC
30 March 2015